LEGACY OF A REFUGEE

AN AMERICAN-HUNGARIAN ENTREPRENEUR'S JOURNEY TO SILICON VALLEY AND BEYOND

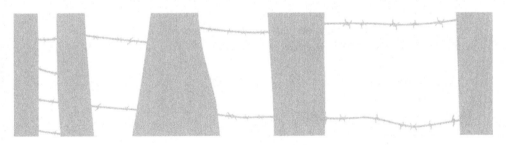

Laszlo Meszaros

with Nancy Eckerson
and Erika Meszaros Wayo

BUFFALO
HERITAGE
UNLIMITED

Buffalo Heritage Press
266 Elmwood Avenue, #407
Buffalo, NY 14222
www.BuffaloHeritage.com

ISBN: 978-1-942483-20-5 (softcover)
ISBN: 978-1-942483-21-2 (hardcover)
ISBN: 978-1-942483-22-9 (e-book)

Library of Congress control number available upon request.

Printed in the U.S.A.

10 9 8 7 6 5 4 3 2 1

CONTENTS

FOREWORD — v

PART ONE | **THE FIRST SEVENTEEN YEARS** — 1

One — Childhood — 3

Two — Communist Hungary — 12

Three — The Escape Plan — 22

Four — Austria Welcomes the Gang of Runaways — 27

Five — All Aboard! — 36

PART TWO | **AMERICA** — 39

Six — Landing in America — 41

Seven — My New Home: Buffalo, New York — 46

Eight — Working in America — 49

Nine — Early Social Life in Buffalo — 58

PART THREE | **MY PROFESSIONAL JOURNEY** — 71

Ten — The Roswell Park Years — 73

Eleven — Triumphant Return to Hungary — 81

Twelve — Knowing When to Move On — 85

Thirteen — The Com-Pro Years — 92

Fourteen — First Steps to Silicon Valley — 111

Fifteen — Doing Business in Hungary – Take Two — 130

PART FOUR | **MESZAROS INTERNATIONAL CENTER OF ENTREPRENEURSHIP (M.I.C.E.)** — 133

PART FIVE | **MY PERSONAL JOURNEY** — 143

Sixteen — Family — 145

Seventeen — Extended Family — 165

REFLECTIONS — 175

ACKNOWLEDGEMENTS — 177

APPENDIX — 183

M.I.C.E. Testimonials — 183

INDEX — 193

FOREWORD

How is it that a seventeen-year old Hungarian refugee can land in New York City with only a dollar and just a few words of English, create multiple successful businesses, selling both of them for millions of dollars, and ultimately find himself serving as Vice President of Business Development for Intel Corporation, one of the most powerful companies on the planet?

What follows is an answer to that question. It's the story of a remarkable individual and gifted businessman, Laszlo (Les) Meszaros.

I've known Les for twenty-five years. I've worked for him, served on boards with him, invested with him and served as his partner in a high-technology startup. I've also sat with him at his kitchen table, drinking the wines he makes, talking for hours about all manner of things he's passionate about. His friends and family have all welcomed my wife and me into the Meszaros family and, by extension, into the Hungarian-American community in Buffalo. I've had the privilege of watching his children grow up. I've attended weddings and wakes. I've argued with him ferociously about some things, and I've helped him fight his battles. He's been as close to me as a brother.

It's always been a privilege, and I count him as one of my dearest friends. Obviously, I was honored when he asked me to contribute a few words to his story.

Most books about successful businessmen are written by someone else and tell the story of that person from a distance. That's not the case here. This is Les' story, as told in his own words. That's appropriate. He's the only person who can do justice to his story, and it's best that the reader experience Les' amazing career as only he can tell it.

Les is a complicated and brilliant individual, but, above all, he is completely fearless, and that's the trait that has allowed him to thrive as an entrepreneur here in the United States.

It's no surprise that he's so tough. As a young boy, he was forced to witness, first-hand, the horrors of war, as the Russian Army marched through his country pushing the Germans back to Berlin. We read about these things in books, but Les lived through them, and it shaped his survival mentality from a very early age.

Americans tend to think of the German surrender as the end of the war. That wasn't the case for Les. It marked the beginning of a savage and oppressive occupation of his beloved Hungary by the Soviet regime. In truth, Les spent almost all of his first sixteen years on a battlefield, either under the control of Nazi Germany or the USSR.

You either survive these experiences or you don't and Les not only survived, he also matured very quickly and assumed the mantle of leadership in order to take care of his family and friends.

By the time he was a teenager, he'd seen enough and done enough for a lifetime. He'd been hardened by the experience, but somehow he never lost his hopes for the future – dreams of independence, control over his own destiny, and economic success.

To pursue his dreams, he risked his life. In 1955, he organized an opportunity so he and two of his closest friends could escape their beloved Hungary, crossing the iron curtain including minefields, barbed-wire fencing and patrolled areas known as borderland "No Man's Land," into free Austria.

I've had the privilege of going to Hungary with Les, visiting his village and standing on the plot of land that once was called "No Man's Land." I've had the opportunity to see what he saw every day. However, I'll never have the ability to see it with his eyes. I do know that getting out of Hungary and into Austria involved enormous risk, courage, self-confidence, and faith in God. I know he left family and friends behind – presumably forever. I know he walked through a minefield where not too many others had made it. I know he was shot at. I know he injured his back serving as a bridge for his friends going over the barbed-wire double fence. I know one of his good friends didn't make it.

But these are just facts to me. For Les, this is the core of his being. It's what made him who he is. What I do know, and what I've suggested to Les, is the obvious: the very first act of entrepreneurial behavior on his part was the day he went over the wire, starting his journey towards America. He's strangely modest about this, and I think I can guess at some of the reasons, but I do stand by my analysis. For every person like Les, there are thousands who opted to stay behind.

Once in the United States, the cab ride itself is an experience. Enough time has passed since the fall of Berlin and the end of the war in Europe that many of us have forgotten that the totalitarian regimes of the era were working very hard to purge certain ethnic and religious minorities from very large regions of Europe. Growing up in Hungary during World War II and then during the Soviet occupation meant that Les grew up in a region where most of the traditional minority groups—Jews, Gypsies and wealthy families—had been either purged or relocated (Laszlo's family among them). New York was completely different. The city was bustling with people of all nationalities and races. Just at a glance, it was obvious the myth was true. This was the place where anyone with some ambition could make a life for themselves.

Les did what all newly-landed immigrants should do. He worked, and he worked hard. He started working dirty and dangerous menial positions. With every job that he took, he worked day and night until he'd advanced as far as possible and learned as much as he could. And then he moved on to a new challenge, many times sacrificing some of his salary in exchange for a new opportunity. While doing all this he also went to night school to improve his English and learn a bit about American culture and values.

This is a pattern in his career. In these early years, Les wasn't at all afraid of being out of work, preferring instead to push himself forward at every opportunity. Les didn't view a job the way most people do. In his mind, jobs are an opportunity to learn and to leverage yourself to the next step. Every job he took he saw as a learning process, whether he was washing dishes, sweeping floors, doing hard labor in a factory, cleaning animal cages, or having an office job somewhere in a big corporation. And, as you might guess, evenings weren't for relaxing. As Les pushed his way through his career, he also pushed his way through college. It took twelve years, but he ultimately earned a Bachelor's Degree in Business Administration.

When Les was asked if he "had a plan" upon arrival in the U.S., his response was instantaneous (and probably obvious): "Yes, I want to be a success. I want to be self-sufficient." Les tied the concept of self-sufficiency to his definition of success, and it's obvious that this is key to the entrepreneurial mindset. He was never looking for anyone to take care of him – he simply wanted the

opportunity to do it himself, and America was the place where he could best express his ambition.

It took years before I was able to figure Les out completely. Yes, he's smart, and he's brash and he's fearless. He's a gifted leader and one of the greatest salesmen I've ever worked with. I know most of the stories you're about to read, but I really didn't know that much about his youth and how his experience in war-torn Hungary shaped him, making him the man he is today.

With friends in Heroes' Square in Budapest in 1995. From left to right: Debbie and Bob Fritzinger, Donna Meszaros, Sándor and Erzsi Nagy, and me.

In the mid-1990s, my wife and I spent a week on vacation in Hungary with Les and his wife, Donna. By this time, the Berlin Wall and the Iron Curtain had fallen and the Soviet Union had collapsed. Freedom and the free market had come to Hungary.

One day, Les drove us all to the village where he grew up. I stood with him on the lot where his childhood home had stood. The property is very near the Austrian border and, during the Soviet oppression; everything behind it was bulldozed so the minefield and the fences could be built. He talked quite a bit about how frustrating it had been for him to be able to see a free Austria while having to live under the oppression of Soviet troops.

The impact of being there, hearing it all and seeing it all first hand, was overwhelming. He told me with tears in his eyes the details of how he and his friends escaped. We stood together and looked at the land border and into Austria and what, for him, was freedom. We talked at length about the challenges he had to overcome to learn the language and the culture of his newly adopted country. He spoke with great pride of the day he swore the oath of citizenship, five years after landing in the U.S.

That day in Hungary, I came to understand just how hard he had struggled to work his way past menial labor, to white collar management and, finally, to owning his own businesses. The challenges he faced are almost unimaginable to me, but it was obvious that he had never lost his faith and never lost track of his vision. It was then that a full picture formed in my mind. I suddenly understood who Les is and what drives him.

He is a remarkable man, and his is a remarkable story.

Robert H. Fritzinger
August 2015

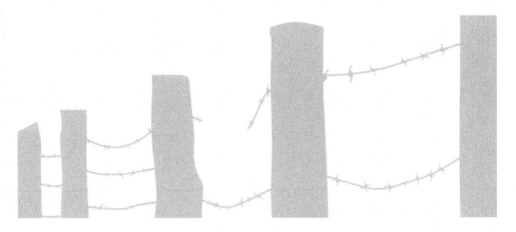

PART ONE

THE FIRST
SEVENTEEN YEARS

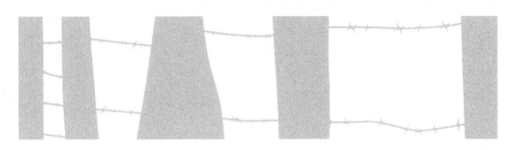

ONE | CHILDHOOD

I, Laszlo Meszaros, better known as Les, was born on April 11, 1939, in the city of Csorna, Hungary. My parents were Erzsébet Kúti and László Mészáros.

My mother died from tuberculosis seven or eight months after I was born. My grandmother took over my care, and later handed me off to my father's sister, Katalin Mészáros, who was unmarried. I was raised by my grandmother and Aunt Kata, until my father re-married in 1942.

My father, who was born in 1900, was an educated man; he graduated from college with a degree in economics. He was also the epitome of a gentleman. He was highly respected, intelligent, brave, wise, kind, compassionate, courteous, and fair in all his interactions. Moreover, he was honest, patient, and he loved my sisters, Klári and Ildi, and me openly and dearly.

Erzsébet Kúti, my birth mother, and my father, László Mészáros, circa 1938.

I was two years old when my father re-located us to Szentpéterfa, Vas County, near the Austrian border. Count Paly (Gróf Erdődy Pál) had an expansive lordship there, and my father had been hired to work for

My baby picture, taken in 1940.

him as an agronomist, working with plants and crops for yielding the best production from the land.

With my sister Klári in 1941.

My sister Klári was three years old when our mother died, and so she has a few memories of her, though not many, because our mother spent most of the time following my birth prior to her death in a sanatorium with tuberculosis.

While my father worked for Count Paly, (Gróf Erdődy Pál) where he was partly responsible for the distribution of parcels of land and forest to the farmers, he came to know a man named Bertalan Schleifer. True, my father was a hard worker, but I think he was also lonely. Bertalan hunted on the Count Paly land and my father also liked hunting, so the two became friends. Bertalan Schleifer, was a forestry engineer, who carried great authority. In fact, when Bertalan died at age 103, he was the oldest forestry engineer living at that time in Hungary.

Because of their friendship, my father met Bertalan's daughter, Margit, and decided to marry her so his children would have a mother. My father brought his new wife to live with us when I was about three. I will never forget when she arrived at Szentpéterfa with a big horse-drawn carriage full of furniture. She was riding, hidden behind the furniture, shaking in fear like most people living here . . . this was, after all, wartime. But just as the carriage pulled up to our house, she stuck her head out to peek at her new home. That was my first glimpse of her.

She warmed up to us right away. From almost the first day, I referred to her as my mother. She was high-spirited, hardworking, nurturing, and had amazing strength and determination. She was also brave and wise, and warmed the hearts of everyone she met.

My new mother was from Tarótfa. The Schleifer family had a large orchard, where we kids enjoyed all kinds of fruit. My new, very strict grandmother was so obsessive in her frugality that she ordered me, her little grandson, to whistle every single moment that I was in the cherry tree picking cherries for her.

She would sit under the cherry tree, snacking on a sandwich, yelling, "Keep whistling, you little bastard!" while I was picking cherries relentlessly. For three to four hours at a time, I did nothing but pick cherries and whistle. Why, you ask? Because while I was whistling, I couldn't possibly be eating up her profits. Now that's strict, and I don't recommend this as a procedure in any of your businesses today.

My step-mother, Margit, and my father during the 1950s.

I was raised in Szentpéterfa, a village with 1,500 residents. Other than my teacher and my family, nearly everybody who lived in Szentpéterfa was of Croatian heritage. Although most could speak Hungarian, they still spoke in Croatian, because that was their mother tongue.

When we arrived, we were the only other family, after the teacher, who knew only Hungarian. We had a hard time, initially, assimilating into the Croatian culture and country life of Szentpéterfa.

Among the adult villagers, we were treated as noble children, but sometimes the other children would mock and tease us for our status and our language. However, because my father carried serious authority, with many people depending on him, it was not long before we were accepted and even began to feel loved.

My father was a true gentleman and my mother was a genuine noblewoman. They were always looking out for others, and thus they became favorites in the village. Today, we call this effective networking techniques and good business practices, but above all, they were good-hearted people. The villagers brought us everything from geese to pork, expressing their gratitude for my father's goodness. It was not easy to fit in with the Croatians, especially for us children, although with the encouragement of our parents, we successfully managed it.

I was motivated to learn the Croatian language by my desire to be accepted by all the kids in the village. I spent many hours studying their language, but even after all that work I was not fluent, so the older kids mocked me and excluded me from their group. It was very painful, and I resolved to work even harder at learning the language. I refused to let language be a barrier. I accelerated the learning process, and after much struggle, I eventually became one of the most popular kids in the village.

Casualties of War

When I was five years old, the Second World War spilled into our area. My childhood was cut short, my innocence lost.

During the war, in the absence of my father who had been drafted, my mother decided that we needed to move temporarily to a safe place.

It was during the first part of 1945, that we moved to Bükks. Today this is a deserted German village in Vas County, in the Körmendi Township, a few miles north of the town of Csákánydoroszló in the wine region. Within the village limits, there was an old farmstead up in the mountains, which you could only get to through the valley. The Russians were pushing the Germans back through Hungary. They were approaching our village through the Bükks Mountains, as they marched back to Austria and then Germany. Numerous families had escaped to Bükks because it was considered safe. Relatives had told my mother that this place was safer than Szentpéterfa, and we would not be found while the Russians were pursuing the Germans. Soon enough, we all found out that really wasn't the truth.

One day, without warning, down in the valley, a troop of Germans appeared. All of the residents of the farm huddled together in the old riverbed, which served as a trench. To our surprise, we discovered that the German soldiers were, in fact, very kind. They gave out candy and bubble gum to the children, and departed quickly to return to their own country. After all, they were retreating from the Russians. Only later, did the shocking news of the Názis' dreadful incinerators and other brutalities reach us.

The Russians arrived just a few hours later, though, compared to the Germans, they were quite barbaric. I, being just a child, could not comprehend what was happening, but I watched them as they ascended from the valley, in search of nothing but food, alcohol, and *barisnya* (women).

And this is how things went. The poor mothers hid wherever they could: under the dresser, on top of a haystack, in the stables with cows, in the bushes. Some of them would even hide in the lavatory, because back in those days we used an outhouse. There was only one bathroom on the farmstead, which we termed *Angol-véce*, a British toilet, that had running water, and by running water, I mean there was a big container placed on a tree, which they filled with water that was then piped to the toilet and used as needed.

Any of the women who did not have the chance to hide, along with those who were discovered in these hideaways, were captured by the Russians and raped in full view of everybody. This was a horrific scene for anyone to witness, much less all of us children. As young ones, we did not understand any of it. Luckily, at the first Russian invasion of the farmstead, my mother managed to hide herself, so she did not have to endure this horror.

After the Russians departed, my mother told me to sit down with her. She had the Bible in her hands—she was always reading the Bible—and explained to me what had just happened. I can say this . . . God and the Bible became life sustaining for my mother and I. She said, "Son, I am sorry that you are forced to grow up at such a young age! You are not quite six years old, but you now have to become a man."

I did not know what she meant by this, but she continued talking to me about it, and then tasked me with a huge assignment. "As the oldest boy in the group," she told me, "you will have to climb to the top of a tree and watch to see when the Russian troops approach. If you see that they are coming up from the valley, you must run as fast as your legs will carry you back to me, so I can warn the women, and then they can hide in time."

This is how I became, at such a tender age, the person in charge. I took it as a huge responsibility, and I was very proud. I was also scared and terrified. I could not admit to my fears, though, because my mother and all the others had put their faith in me. I could not risk losing their confidence. Each day, I would go to the Bükks Mountains and wait and watch.

Day after day, I took my post. Finally, it happened. I noticed the Russians approaching from afar, so I ran as fast as I could, screaming, "They're coming, they're coming!" Immediately, everybody ran to hide, including my mother. Once the Russians arrived, they looked everywhere for the women. They climbed on the top of haystacks and searched with their bayonet guns. Despite my early warning, some women were found, all of whom were ravaged. Their yelling and crying still rings in my head, and burns in my memory. Even so many years later, I still have nightmares about it.

One woman was surrounded by twenty-five Russian soldiers, all of whom were half-naked and waiting for their turn. We lost one young woman, who died while she was held down as soldiers raped her, one after another. She died and the maggots did not even notice that they were raping a dead woman. Barbarians . . . this is how these Mongol troops behaved.

I will also never forget the older women dressing up younger women in their clothing, so the younger ones would be mistaken for being elderly. One or two managed to avoid the horrible experience of assault, but most times, the barbarians came, tore their dresses from them, and jumped on them like wild animals.

Being just a child, I could not fully process scenes like these, and yet I cannot forget them either. Even today, when I am having trouble getting to sleep or waking during the night, these scenes flash in front of me, as vividly as when they actually occurred. I did not understand rape at that age, but now that I understand what it all means, these memories hold even more horror.

When the Russians finally left, a grand idea came to me, as though God himself had sent me a message. For many nights, I lay awake thinking about how I could save my mother from these fiends. Up until then she had narrowly avoided assault, but what would happen the next time? Suddenly, I knew what had to be done to save her.

With one of my friend's help, I made a hole in the side of one of the haystacks the size of a small door, big enough for our mothers to hide in. From some old wooden planks we fashioned a door, then covered it with hay, as evenly as the haystack itself, and placed it over the hole so the Russians would not notice it. From the outside, no one could tell that it was a door.

I told my mother what we had done, and she replied, "Lacika (pronounced Lot-see-ka, a term of endearment, like a nickname, for László), this is very good, this will work well."

Then I thought of something else. "How are you going to breathe while in there?"

"Listen," she replied, "behind that creek there are some elder trees. These branches are almost hollow. There is just some spongy material inside that you can dig out." I followed her instructions, and cut the branches down with my pocketknife. We cleaned out the insides using a little stick to push the soft parts through. Just as she planned, they were able to use them to breathe while inside the haystack.

Then came the real test. The next time the Russians came, I was waiting in the treetop. As soon as I noticed that they were approaching, I rushed back to the farmstead to warn everybody. I was a nervous wreck, afraid that they would find my mother despite our precautions. But, thank God, that did not happen, although they began showing up nearly every day, raping any women they could find. The poor victims tried to hide from them, but these cold-blooded barbarians found them anyway. I still feel shivers run down my back when I recall those days.

Later on in life, after so many nightmare experiences, I wondered how I kept my courage and strength during those times. Instead of falling to pieces because of all the horror, I found myself growing into a man. I wonder, in times of danger, if the rational problem-solving skills are automatically activated. I have always been able to utilize this feature of the human mind throughout my entire life; I find that I am able to turn down the panic and turn on my problem-solving skills during times of danger and stress.

After a while, fewer and fewer Russians and Germans arrived. However, a rearguard arrived, and stayed with us for a while because we had food and water. I should mention that these soldiers were not hungry for women; instead, these soldiers brought great quantities of alcohol with them and were constantly drunk.

The residents of the farmstead stuck together; we had become a large family. We held hands, consoled each other, and prayed together. There was some kind of unrest in the air, though. I still felt that I was responsible for the others, so I constantly ran around among the soldiers, watching who did what, who had a gun, and who was drunk, hoping I could warn everybody to be careful. There was nobody else willing to do this, and I had no fear left in me at that point. However, all of my spying and dodging didn't do anything to stop them from committing the most heinous crime ever.

One night, we were having dinner around the kitchen table. While we were saying our prayers, two soldiers entered the room, both holding guns. Thoroughly drunk, they were singing, laughing, and playing with their weapons. One of them approached a young woman, who was sitting directly next to me, holding her baby in her arms – as she had just finished breastfeeding the infant. On my other side sat my mother, my younger sister, Ildi, and my older sister, Klári.

Without warning, the soldier grabbed the baby from his mother's arms, and threw him up towards the ceiling. God only knew what he was saying in Russian, but he kept on throwing and catching the baby, while the poor mother cried and begged for her child. I tried to console her; she was clutching me desperately. Finally, this monster pulled his gun while the baby was in the air and shot him through the head. His brains splattered all over the table. The dead baby landed on the floor, with the soldier laughing because he had shot the poor child.

I will forever remember the unholy howl that rose up from the mother's throat, just before she collapsed. Everybody began to panic and wail, while many others fainted. I was momentarily powerless, hanging on to the young mother as we both sobbed and trembled. I also tried to console my mother and those around us, all of whom were paralyzed from shock. I have never been able to forget this tragic event. I have seen it in front of me almost every day since; I just cannot erase it from my mind.

Several minutes after the shooting occurred, while we were weeping and praying together, a Russian officer entered the kitchen, and started arguing with the soldiers. The murderer's companion told him what happened, whereupon the officer pulled out his gun and shot dead the heartless swine who had killed the infant. I felt no remorse; the bastard deserved it.

This all happened within a half an hour's time, but a whole lifetime isn't long enough to forget it. I was never able to understand how one human could do this to another. Because of all I had seen and been through, I was forced to put my childhood behind me and grow up right then and there.

Another day brought more horror still. Our elderly men in the village would fish in the nearby creek, bringing home the fish they caught so we would have something to eat. On this particular day, one of the old men was carrying the twelve or so fish he caught in a kettle. A soldier demanded that he throw the fish into the British toilet, so they would stay alive in that water. Since the soldier did not know how the English lavatory worked, he flushed the toilet, causing most of the fish to be flushed away. He then started screaming at the old man, and shot him in the head, killing him. I was dumbfounded and speechless.

The elderly man had always been a favorite in our town. His name was Gyuri-bá (George); he was a kind-hearted, good man, and now he was dead because of this brutal Russian's ignorance. These soldiers, if I am not mistaken, were Mongols, and were so primitive that they would spread shoe polish on a slice of bread, then eat it. They did the same with toothpaste, or sometimes they gobbled the whole tube of toothpaste, all by itself.

Whenever I think back on that time, I can only remember the misery and pain, because a child should not have to endure such things. Of course, no one should, and most people are lucky enough never to have to witness anything like this in their lives, thank God.

This was my life's most tragic period. This was when I learned what suffering means, and that one must respect people and value human life. I learned how painful it is to lose a child, and what it really means to love each other, as instructed in the Ten Commandments: "Love your neighbors as yourself." This is when I realized that life is not "child's play." I would never have the chance to learn what "child's play" was, however, because after the war, the era of communism arrived in Hungary, and brought suppression, injustice, torture, killing, and unhappiness to the lives of many.

I endured many terrible experiences while still a child, and I feel bad for everyone who suffered and was tortured during this terrible time. However, when I think back, I must say that I also learned a lot from these experiences, and they gave me a direction in life, one I may not have not taken otherwise. Maybe this is when I developed the desire to become a doctor, to help people, to do good for people. In Hungary, physicians were looked up to . . . like God!

Return to our Home in Szentpéterfa

To the best of my recollection, sometime around 1945, the soldiers stopped showing up, and the Army retreated, it seemed like the war had ended. We gathered our belongings, and a man with his mule-drawn wagon took us—my mother, my sisters, and me—home. When we returned to Szentpéterfa, we were amazed to see that we still had our house. With all the joy and relief imaginable, we stepped over the threshold of our home once more.

We prayed every single day for our father's return, since he was still off at war. It wasn't until later that we discovered he had been captured by the Russians and held in Russia. From there, he managed to successfully escape, walking for forty-five days back to Hungary, and finally home. One night, at around four in the morning, there was a knock on the window. My mother jumped out of bed and awakened us. Our father—tortured, tired, and looking like a skeleton—had returned to his family.

Klári, Ildi, and I nearly jumped out of our skin with happiness. We couldn't stop hugging and kissing him. We cried and cried, out of the sheer relief and joy of having him back again.

I get shivers, even now, as I remember what my father said he endured during the forty-five-day journey home. They were constantly forced to hide out in the wilderness, where they slept on the ground, and ate the meat of dead horses and cats that were left rotting on the side of the road, just so they could survive. He would bring this up time and again throughout his life, that they ate a lot of carrion, and jokingly said that this is when he started liking rat and cat meat. Still, they arrived home in relatively good health, which was a miracle from God.

My father was a great man. The word *Édesapám* (my dear father in Hungarian) is a beautiful word. Unfortunately, the word *Édesanyám* (my dear mother) was one I could never use. God, however, had given me a stepmother who took good care of us. Even though she was very strict, she loved us and raised us so we would become the trustworthy individuals we are today. I respect her for taking on motherless children and raising them. I grew to love her and honored her with the name mother, rather than stepmother.

My father returned to his job, and was able to keep at it until the Communists assumed power and nationalized everything in the country. Between 1945 and 1952, Hungary sustained the worst possible changes ever. The Communists expelled the *Kisgazda Párt* (Smallholder's Party), which Father was a member of, and they completely took over Hungary. They were very dictatorial. They were shrewd, very shrewd. Initially, only the less educated Hungarians signed up for the Communist party, believing the empty promises of the good life that Communism would provide.

TWO | **COMMUNIST HUNGARY**

It turned out to be all propaganda. The truth was, the Communist regime that was then in power confiscated all the assets and property from the people, and most of the farmers' land was nationalized. They were allowed to hold on to a little land however, which they could cultivate for themselves, but such parcels were so small, people could barely make a living from them. The Communists didn't share the wealth; they confiscated the wealth and took control of it. After the nationalization, my father also started to work for the government, where he continued his work as an agronomist, this time subdividing the farmers' formerly large properties into two portions. All but a small portion of each farm was now under the control of the new regime. The economy was called TSZCS, an abbreviation for Collective Farming.

My father did not cozy up to politics, so he was deemed a "reactionary." One night, a big truck appeared on our street with four machine-gun wielding soldiers. They broke into our house; they did not even wait until we could open the door before we heard the Ávós (the secret service police) say, "You are under arrest, get your things. You are being banished from this house. Whatever you own, remains here."

As children we could not comprehend why we had to leave our comfortable home in the middle of the night. It was frightening, absolutely frightening. Mom and Dad were running here and there, trying to gather up our belongings. These bastards were constantly saying, "No! Leave that!" We had to leave behind personal belongings, photos, and jewelry—which there was little of anyway. Anything that they could not carry on their backs had to stay on the premises.

I cannot even imagine how my poor parents felt, especially my father, when all this was happening. He did not dare to argue with them, because they had guns and he did not want to place his family in danger or, worse, lose them. After all his work, suffering, and attendance to others, everything was still taken away from him. He was about forty-eight years old at that time, and from one day to the next his wealth and his home were confiscated without any explanation. My mother just prayed silently and did what she was told.

Back when my father was still working for Count Paly, he had a servant who took care of the house, drove the carriages, and looked after the horses, among other tasks. My parents treated him and his family very well, as though they were part of our own family. They couldn't have had any complaints about working for the Count's right-hand man. When my father suddenly became a "reactionary," his servant, named Gábor Pongrác, immediately joined the Communist party. He had no education, could barely read or write, and was not at all intelligent, but it was men like him who became the first Communists.

We were banished to Pongrác's little house, while he and his family moved into our beautifully furnished house, with three bedrooms and a beautiful garden. How ironic! Sadly, the Pongrác family seemed to have no memory of all the kindnesses given to them by both of my parents. They lorded their new position over them. They were now the big shots.

This was an unimaginable trial for my father and the entire family. There were the three of us children, Klári, Ildi and myself. And, to make matters worse, Ildi, who was born prematurely, had serious health issues. On several occasions, we had to call the doctor, and I was always the one asked to fetch him.

The city of Szombathely was about fifteen miles from us, and this was the closest place to go to find a doctor or a hospital. I vividly remember that whenever we needed the doctor, I would travel to the city taking two bikes, so that one could be used by the doctor. When the doctor's visit was over, I would have to ride back with him, another fifteen miles each way, to bring the bike back home.

It was not easy for my poor father to support us at this time. Luckily, he could still work with forestry and the state farms because he had an education and they needed his expertise. He rode his bike every day to Szombathely and the other farms, in summer and in winter. He worked for the state for several years, until he retired.

Because of my father, we children were also declared "reactionaries," which caused a lot of mean-spiritedness and bullying, especially at the school in Szentpéterfa. The old teachers had been replaced by new Communist teachers who used us to express their hatred for "reactionaries."

I was their main target; they made me remove the religious-themed pictures from the classroom walls, and if I did not do what they asked of me, they made me kneel on an old, dry ear of corn in the corner of the room. They routinely humiliated me because I was a "willful, self-asserted" little boy. When these teachers found me in church, they punished me and made fun of me in front of the other students. They made me take down all the crosses and religious icons, a punishment that troubled me.

The teachers also forbade us to go to church, even though we were raised very religiously by our parents. Before the Communists took over, we went to church every morning. During elementary school, we started the day early with prayers and gave thanks to God for keeping us alive and for giving us another day. This all ended when the Communists took over. We had to follow the new rules and laws, which were all anti-religious. We could only go to church in secret; we could not talk about politics at home; and we had to praise the Communists and express belief in everything they said.

Szentpéterfa, Hungary. Top to bottom: the border, my church, and the school I attended.

The 1950s were probably the worst period in the history of Hungary. This is when everything under the sun was nationalized. All the grain, vegetables, fruit, and domestic animals the land yielded had to be handed over to the state. The farmers could keep only a small portion of it. Most of the daily milk was commandeered, so there was barely any left for the family. To add insult to injury, the farmers had to surrender and transport these goods to a central agency themselves. Even though everybody worked his own land and grew his own food, we still had to go to Szombathely for bread. Above and beyond the food that grew in the ground, the farmers had to give up most of their animals, too.

When I returned home from America for the first time, I got into an argument with an old school Communist. I pressed him as to why you couldn't buy veal anywhere in Hungary. He said that veal isn't available in Hungary because the Hungarian people don't like veal. What a joke! I was very close to hitting him, but my sister Klári prevented me, which was a good thing, as I would have been immediately sent to prison.

Over the years, my father always encouraged me to "Just do it, work hard, be trustworthy, and you will be rewarded for it." He was very sad because of the situation we faced, even though he had nothing to do with causing it. I always think of my father with admiration. He, who went through so much, instead of giving in like most men did back then, encouraged us to hold on. He showed us how to be strong and to have faith in God. My father taught us to be wise, to be of clean conscience, and to never quit. His words fortified and empowered me to never give up no matter what happened.

Peer Pressure

Growing up with my siblings in this Croatian village, I had to take on the customs of the local kids and adapt to their way of life. My younger sister and I eventually were able to fit in.

Fitting in also meant that I work side-by-side with the other boys. I tilled the soil and cleaned the stables with them and we worked together at the threshing. There was also some misbehavior, and I felt I had to participate in that, as well.

My family only had a small house. We did not have any farmland, just a little vegetable garden and a few chickens. But, during that time, I tended to the more than a hundred pigeons that I was raising. My mother often used pigeon meat to make an excellent Sunday soup. Sometimes, on a Sunday morning, my job was to go out and shoot two pigeons. This caused me real heartache, because each pigeon was dear to me. I had named them all, and they would fly to my outstretched hands and talk to me in their own language. I also raised rabbits in the back of the stable so we would have some other kind of meat every once in a while.

My father was beloved by the people of the village because he was the one who treated them fairly when he distributed land. So, even though it caused them great hardship, people always brought us presents, from eggs to meat and poultry. They took care of us, something that deeply touched me, because it was surprising to see how much they valued my family. Because of this, I always helped the old farmers with the fieldwork. And, to be honest, I also liked the fact that they accepted me and treated me as an equal.

I knew that my father was an employee of the state, earning minimum wage. We almost never had money to ride the Ferris wheel, for ice cream, or for other things children enjoy. Saint Péter and Paul's Day in Szentpéterfa took place on June 29th every year. Every year my poor father gave us his last pennies so my sisters and I could participate in the festivities and have a good time.

Mostly, though, I lived the life of any young boy in the village. My older sister, on the other hand, never was able to assimilate into the fabric of the village. After sixth grade, she moved to Szombathely to live with Aunt Kata, who we called *Nénje*. She was one of my father's six sisters and the one who helped raise us after the death of our mother.

Klári was a very attractive, blond-haired girl. She resembled our mother and had many admirers, but she never learned Croatian and did not like living in the village. When she came home for a weekend visit once or twice a month, all the boys would hang out around our house. They offered me cigarettes to bring Klári out of the house because they all wanted to talk to her. I took advantage of the situation and was never short of cigarettes. I was able to arrange a few dates, but my sister was never really interested, and she was a little haughty because she lived in the city. I asked her to be more polite to them because we were still living in the village and had to blend into the community. Klári moved away to continue school and eventually became a nurse.

I continued to grow up. The boys next door, and other village boys, made up my group of friends. There was a small group of boys that played pranks, and I, of course, joined in. We did some ugly things. Now, when I think back, I feel ashamed and regret those deeds. I don't even know what we were thinking. We played many pranks on the households where pretty girls lived. For example, in the middle of the night we would wheel a family carriage from a yard, take it apart, bring it into the stable, then put it back together, filled with horse and cow manure, and leave it there. The poor farmers had to wake up at five o'clock in the morning to go to work in the fields, only to find their carriages were misplaced. They sure had some trouble those days.

Other times, we would take a different carriage apart, put the pieces on top of a haystack, put it back together again, and then leave it there, having hidden the ladder.

Sometimes our mischievous acts would backfire, however. One of the boys, who knew that we did not have hens (it was difficult to get ahold of eggs back then), said: "Here, I will show you how you can get eggs." We went to the neighbor's late at night, found the place where the hens laid eggs, then picked up the eggs and carried them away in our shirts. We learned to be quick.

One time, I was wearing a very good shirt, and had collected a dozen or so eggs. When we were stealing the last of the eggs, we were spotted by one of the old men so we had to run away quickly. But we could not run on the street, we had to run through the backyards, following a path where we would not be seen. This is where the sheds were, and where the carts were stored with their shafts sticking out into the pathway. In my hurry, I crashed into one of these, and broke all the eggs inside my shirt. Naturally, my shirt, pants, and body were covered with the egg mess.

Even though the old man did not catch us, everybody knew who belonged to this band of hooligans. At home, I had to hide my shirt and clean myself, which was not an easy task, especially in that small house. I tried as hard as I could to conceal what I had done, but my mother realized that something was wrong. My father was asleep by then, but the next day my mother asked me about the night before. I initially denied everything, but then admitted to it, saying that I was only thinking of my family when I stole the eggs. My mother pulled out our Bible and explained to me, "No matter what your reason is, stealing is stealing," and told me that I must never do that again.

When my father came home from work that afternoon, she told him everything. He was extremely angry with me and pulled off his belt to whip me. I fled to the back of our garden, where he chased me for a while. In the end, he got ahold of me and gave me a few lashes to set me straight. It was a rough lesson.

The Budding Entrepreneur

During this time, I kept thinking that I had to devise a way to make some money. A friend and I decided that right before Christmas we would cut down Christmas trees in secret and sell them. We found some to chop down, tied them together, put them in a sack, attached them to our bicycles, and walked them up to Szombathely, where we kept them hidden until Aunt Nénje sold them "under the table" to trustworthy acquaintances.

We did this for about two weeks before Christmas. This was done in secret, because we were not allowed to buy a Christmas tree—all religious activities were forbidden, even the festive ones. Because of this, everybody did everything "under the table." We left the trees at Aunt Nénje's place, where she sold them to her friends. I told my father where I was going, and what I was doing, so he would know what was happening when I escaped from my bed in the middle of the night, only to return at the crack of dawn.

In the beginning, he was dead set against my Christmas tree business, but later he said, "Look, son. This Communist system forces us to do illegal things. With your scheme, you are not causing harm to anybody; moreover you've brought some happiness to those who wouldn't have been able to get a Christmas tree otherwise." My father's approval really meant a lot to me. So we kept on selling Christmas trees, and we managed to make a little pocket money for ourselves. Although the Communists forbade any religious associations, these Christian traditions were so important to the locals that they would risk everything to keep these customs alive.

I also devised other methods of making money. In Szentpéterfa, and in other villages too, people mixed manure with clay to hold the substrate together. They used this compound to build houses. We made pretty good money by collecting manure and selling it to builders. Besides this, I also worked as a helper for the peasants who operated the threshing machines, and did other things as well. I can honestly say that I have done almost everything under the sun to earn money. Even back then, I knew that diligence was necessary for survival and advancement. Money is not everything, but without money, it is impossible to maintain a decent life.

The school years flew by in Szentpéterfa, and my Croatian was getting very good. Those days in Szentpéterfa bring back plenty of nice memories. We lived in unity; everybody loved and respected each other, and even though there was some envy and wickedness, our village was ultimately a really, lovely place. Friday, Saturday, and Sunday nights, we boys and girls of the town entertained ourselves by walking back and forth through the village singing Hungarian and Croatian songs. We conversed and flirted together. We really came to love each other; it was a true group of friends.

Trouble is Brewing

One of the issues in the villages back then was that age difference mattered a lot. A boy could only hang out with boys of his own age group. Somebody a year or two younger was deemed a "child." The girls also preferred dating guys who were a few years older than they were.

This was a problem because I liked a girl from Szentpéterfa who was a year older than I was. The older boys literally forbade me to date her, even though she liked me, as well. In those days, if you disobeyed the older boys, you got "the shit" beaten out of you.

Dating at that age only involved talking outside the house at the gate and holding hands. The only time it made sense to flirt was in the evening, in the dark, when you just might have the chance to kiss her . . . or touch her hand. So while I was living in Szentpéterfa, this was how I "dated": I held a few girls' hands, hugged them, sang along with them while walking down the street, chatted with them, took them to the Pinka (a little river behind the village) to swim, and rode them on the handlebars of my bike. We were content with the simplicity of those days, but I readily admit, I was only content for a while.

As the years rolled by, I realized that the rowdy group I was spending time with was not for me. My father had even threatened me because of them, urging me to disassociate myself from them and find another crowd of friends. By the time I reached the eighth grade, I had matured a lot.

I completed elementary school with good grades, and then had to decide where to go to further my education. My father really wanted me to study and go to a *gimnázium* (an academically-oriented high school), but I loved life in the country and didn't really want to move away for school. My father kept pestering me, though, and ultimately begged me to do it for his sake and for my future. So I agreed.

Only a few of the youngsters left the village to go to beyond elementary school and on to high school. Most of the boys stayed home to work in the fields; the girls got married, had children, and lived their oppressed lives. That year there were only two boys and two girls from Szentpéterfa who applied to the *gimnázium* in Szombathely. Of the four of us, they accepted three, rejecting only one application: mine, because I was still considered a "reactionary." This made my father grim. I was not too sad, however, because I did not really want to go away to school in Szombathely. But my father kept pushing the matter until three months into the school year I was accepted at the Nagy Lajos Gimnázium in Szombathely.

I lived in the school dorms, and I can still recall how every morning we had to form a soldiers' line while walking to school. Along the way, we had to sing Soviet and Hungarian marching songs. The first was always the song entitled: "*Elnyomás, szolgasors, ez volt a rend ezer évig*" (Repression, slave destiny, it was the order of thousands of years).

Because I started school three months late, I was quite behind and worried about catching up. I had a Russian language teacher who picked on me from the very beginning because he knew that I had been found to be a "reactionary." He warned me from the get-go that I could be good in geography and math; I could catch up to or even surpass my classmates in those subjects, but I would have a hard time with Russian, so I should not be surprised if he failed me.

I told him: "Let's try it, and we will see what happens." He did not know that I was fluent in Croatian, and Croatian and Russian are very similar, especially in their pronunciation. On the exam at the end of the first year, I received the highest grade, which really bothered my teacher because he could not fail me as he promised. This teacher, a Communist, always spied on students to catch them going to church, and knew my parents' political leanings, so it was no surprise that I had a target on my back at school.

The first year at the *gimnázium* went quite well. I caught up in everything, my grades were good, and I was the only one from my class who got an A in Russian—so I was pretty proud of myself. During the summer, I lived at home in Szentpéterfa, where I took a few odd jobs so I could contribute to my family's budget. I found time to have fun too. I loved loafing about in the village, singing with friends, and chasing girls. We put on plays at our cultural center, so we had a good time without ever being bored.

When the second year of high school arrived, I moved back to the dorm in Szombathely. My studies went better that year since I had started school at the same time as everybody else. I was a good student, and Russian continued to be a "piece of cake" for me. However, problems began when the second year final exams came around.

Back in those days, students not only had to take verbal exams in everything they learned that year, but also on material from the year before, to make sure they had not forgotten what they had learned in the previous year. I agreed with this system, although it was really difficult to get through the exams. But what does life consist of if not hardship? I was becoming an expert at handling challenges.

The Price of a Prayer

I had one really good pal, also from Szentpéterfa, and together we decided that before the exams, we would go to church to ask God for help. Because it was forbidden, the only way we could go was if we could somehow escape from the dorm. The only time religious ceremonies were held was on Sunday mornings. To add another obstacle to prevent students from going to church, they created a busy schedule for us. We were awoken at six o'clock and immediately had to play sports. We had breakfast at ten o'clock, and from eleven to two, we had to study. We could go to the city between two o'clock and four, but we had to be back by four o'clock sharp, then study again until five, eat dinner, followed by bathing, after which we went to bed. This is how each day went.

My pal and I had talked to a few of our mutual friends and asked them to help us escape from the room where we studied so we could go to church. And we succeeded. With the help of the other boys, we tied blankets together and used them to climb down from the window. We went to mass, came back, and then whistled for them to lower the blankets so we could climb back to the study room. If a supervisor came by, they told him we were in the bathroom. We did this for several Sundays until, one time, as we turned around after taking communion, who did we see in the first row of the church but the Russian teacher! Yes, the Russian teacher who hated me so much, and who was very happy to have caught us. I knew that I was going to be in some serious trouble. I was shaking in my shoes as I crept back to my dorm.

An hour after we returned to the dormitory, the director sent for us. He called us all sorts of bad things because we were breaking the rules; moreover, we had left school grounds, setting a bad example for the others. In the end, he told us that we were expelled from the dormitory for good, but could remain in the *gimnázium* and finish our studies. I got my things together, and along with my pal, we got on our bikes and rode home feeling depressed, sad, angry, scared, and confused.

I told my parents what had happened, and, fortunately, they understood. My mother told me, "You did the right thing," but my father said that we should have been smarter. He said we still had to finish our exams, and I promised that I would.

We bicycled fifteen miles to and from Szombathely every day for the final exams. Even when the sunny weather changed to snow, rain or strong winds, we kept our word and completed our exams. We both got good grades.

I did not wait for my diploma, however. Alfonz Szoldatits, one of my village friends, and I decided to head west. After discussing our situation over and over again, we concluded there was no future for us in Hungary unless we became part of the Communist party, and this we would not do.

THREE | THE ESCAPE PLAN

My friend Alfonz and I decided that we would try to escape to Austria through what would come to be known as the Iron Curtain—minefields and barbed-wire fences that surrounded the country. We vowed not to stop until we reached America. We had heard stories in the village where I grew up from people who had gone to America before the war and came back to spread the good news about the freedom and wealth in that country. They told us, drilled into us, that America was a dreamland! There was a good life to be had there.

But before I left on the big journey with Alfonz, my pal from school and I decided to go to Szombathely and spy on the Russian teacher who had told on us, so we could take revenge.

I thought it was a brilliant plan. In our house, on one side of the kitchen, there was a room that my mother shared with my sister Ildi. In the first room, which faced the street, I bunked with my father. There were two beds in our room. My father always woke up early and went to bed early, because he was exhausted at the end of the day from riding his bike to and from work. That night, as soon as my father fell asleep, I quietly opened the window and sneaked out.

I got on my bike to meet my pal and together we rode to Szombathely. We followed the teacher as he was returning home from the theater alone, and then we charged him from behind, threw a blanket over him, and beat him up. Not so much that he would die, but enough that he felt real pain. Then we rode our bikes home. He had not seen us, but he suspected us, and reported us, though he had no proof. I was home by midnight. I climbed into the house through the window, jumped into bed and faked a snore.

The next day, two police officers came from Szombathely looking for me. More accurately, they were looking for my father, who was at work in the neighboring village. They started to interrogate my mother, asking questions like, "Where was your son last night?" My mother responded: "Lacika went to bed early, and that is all I know."

When my father arrived home, the police officers were still there, waiting for him. Poor Father, he could barely get off his bike before they asked him, "Where was your son last night?"

My father could only say what he knew. "He slept here with me in this room." They replied immediately that it was impossible, and told him what I was accused of doing.

My father remembered everything that we had talked about regarding the Russian teacher, and the fact that I suffered a lot because of him. He said, "Look, we went to bed at the same time, then what happened to him during the night, whether he flew out of here or not, I do not know. All I know is he was here when I went to bed, and he was here when I woke up. I will talk to my son."

I went out back and hid in a haystack. The police officers left with a promise from my father that he would talk to me, after which they would return for another interrogation. When I emerged from my hiding place, Father started questioning me, and saw immediately that I was being very secretive.

It was obvious that I knew why the police officers were there. I also knew that if my father were caught in a lie, he would receive a beating from the Communists. In those days, if anybody accused you of anything, and you denied it and lied, they beat you until you confessed or had to be taken to the hospital.

It was a barbaric system and I did not want him to get hurt because of me, so I confessed. I told my father what happened, and also explained my reasons. He said, "Between you and me, you are right, but according to the law, one cannot do such things. I will have to call the police in Szombathely, so they can apprehend you and the friend who was there with you."

I could only say, "Father, you are right. Do what you have to do."

By then I had made up my mind about escaping Hungary, so I knew I would not be meeting with any police, unless they caught me at the border. My father did call them, and told them that his son had confessed that he and his friend were the culprits, and asked them when they would be interrogating us. They gave him a date, saying they would be back in two weeks. That was just enough time to plan our escape.

Beyond the Barbed-Wire and Mine Fields

Three of us decided to undertake the journey: Alfonz Szoldatits and István Szoldatits (not related), and me. In the end, only two of us would succeed and we would do this all without our parents' knowledge.

The Hungarian/Austrian border was very closely guarded. Border control soldiers marched back and forth at all times, and there were watchtowers every 650 yards manned by armed, binocular-equipped soldiers, who were continually on the lookout for those who were trying to escape. As communism seeped into the country, they closed all the western borders with double, barbed-wire fences, claiming that it was to prevent western Fascists from entering Hungary. Everybody knew that quite the opposite was the case – they did not want Hungarians to escape to the West.

In front of the double barbed-wire fence there was a seventy-five-yard-long border-zone covered by tall grass. Ditches had been dug and explosives were planted in the ground, tied together with a wire that was invisible to the eye. If someone tripped the wire or got caught on it, the ditch exploded on both sides. In front of the grassy border-zone there was another fifty-five-yard strip of finely ground soil, very similar to sand. If somebody stepped in it, the footprints allowed authorities to identify the shoes or even the individual and provided proof that he or she had attempted to cross the border. In Szentpéterfa, the barbed-wire fence was also strung across the Pinka River, all the way to the bottom of the creek, so one could not risk crossing there.

We decided that we would not go through the river, but across the land instead. We befriended the border control soldiers before our actual escape. They liked the girls from our village and wanted to meet them. The girls from Szentpéterfa were anti-regime and quite proud, however. They did not want to talk to soldiers who they considered the enemy. Because they underwent brainwashing in order to become border guards, these soldiers truly were the enemy.

Befriending the border patrol gave us a great advantage. We found out that they worked three shifts a day, where the shift changes took place, in what part of the village, and at what time of day, because we did not want to cross the border at night, in the pitch dark. We took photographs of some of the village girls and gave these to the border guards, saying that Aranka or Jolánka had asked about them and wanted to meet. Early on a Sunday afternoon, on August 17, 1955, we told the border guards, "Do not wait for your shift change. Leave ten or fifteen minutes early, and go to the village. Here are pictures of the girls who will be waiting for you." The naive men believed us because they were so anxious to meet young women.

We thought we would have about twenty minutes to cross the unguarded portion of the border. Although it was impossible to know what was going on with the guards in the watchtowers, we had no choice. We had to take advantage of the twenty-minute gap we had engineered.

That Sunday afternoon, before we left, I went into my room while my father and mother were napping. I shoved three or four pairs of socks into my pockets, and tucked a few pairs of underwear and a shirt down my pants. This is how I started my great journey to America.

Without even saying good-bye (we knew our parents would be severely punished for withholding knowledge of our plans), the three of us started off. We arrived at that grassy expanse, our first danger zone, and looked at each other, trying to decide who would take that first step onto the minefield. If the first person could successfully avoid the mines, the others could carefully follow.

I thought of myself as a leader, so I volunteered to go first. I had no idea what was in front of me or under me, nor did I know if I was going to trip the wire that connected the mines, or, worse, if I would step on one. Finally, drenched in sweat and shaking like a leaf, I successfully covered the seventy-five yards of minefields. The others followed right behind me, all of us trembling with each step. At that point, we went numb. We had failed to take into account the stretch between the two fences, an area called the "death zone." Crossing was guaranteed death because the explosives were so closely placed that there was no space to walk.

István started to cry, mumbling to himself, "My dear mother, I cannot leave you behind. My dear father, I cannot leave you behind, either. I need to go back; I will not be able to leave you." He turned around and retraced our steps and, thank God, made it back in one piece. We later learned that he was put in prison and was not released until the Revolution of 1956.

Alfonz and I looked at each other, wondering what to do next. "Look, Alfonz," I said. "There is only one solution. I will climb up the Hungarian side of the fence, you will hold my ankles, and I will throw myself to the other side. Then, I will hold onto the barbed-wire on the far side, creating a bridge with my body, so you can slide across my torso to the other side. If they don't shoot us from the watchtowers, everything will be fine."

That is exactly how it happened. I climbed to the top with trembling legs. The barbed-wire was not stable, but I managed to hold onto the column while my friend held my ankles. Then I said, "In the name of God, grant me wings." While in the air, I suddenly needed to figure out how to fit my hands between the spike-like barbs. It was like a scene out of an action movie. Within seconds, my hands were pierced. Grabbing onto the barbed-wire, I forced myself to focus on one thing only—I was seconds away from freedom. Miraculously, stretched there between the fences, bleeding from my palms, I felt no pain.

I shouted to my friend: "Alfonz, hurry up! They're going to start shooting at us!" He slowly slid over me. I kept my body as rigid as possible. Alfonz finally made it to the other side of the border. He turned around, climbed onto the Austrian side of the fence, reached across, and grabbed me by the belt. I did a 360-degree turn so I could leap to the other side, with the barbs digging ever deeper into my hands.

While Alfonz was pulling me through the barbed-wire fence, the guards spotted us from the watchtowers and started to shoot. Hundreds of bullets pinged by us, but God Almighty still needed us on Earth. The rifle shots continued to pour down on us like a monsoon, and, yet, the taste of freedom rocketed us beyond any normal human strength or capability.

What saved us next was the cornfield nearby. It was mid-August so the corn was already nice and tall. We fled into the field and started to crawl under the cover of the cornstalks. They continued to shoot at us, even though the Hungarian soldiers were not allowed to shoot into Austrian territory. Because the guards were held responsible for anyone who successfully escaped through the area they were protecting, they just kept on shooting.

A mosaic of my escape over the barbed-wire Iron Curtain from Hungary to Austria on August 17, 1955.
Illustration By Joseph Wayo.

FOUR | AUSTRIA WELCOMES THE GANG OF RUNAWAYS

Our escape plan worked. We scrambled through the cornfield at an incredible pace and reached the other side. We were finally safe in Austria.

We found ourselves in a big open field, where an Austrian peasant was pitching hay into his carriage. We ran toward him with such speed that we could have won the Olympics. We started to talk to him. We did not speak German, but we were lucky because he was from a community near Szentpéterfa. This was a vineyard called Gorica, and the owners of that vineyard spoke German, Hungarian, and Croatian.

We told him our story and he immediately left the hay behind, put us on his carriage, and took us to his house. He told his wife, who only spoke German, about our situation. They took us in, brought us food and drink, and asked what they could do for us. I told them I had no idea, because I was not familiar with Austrian laws. I did ask if they could bandage my bleeding hands and she immediately honored my wish. Then the man thought for a bit and replied, "Most likely the police will come get you and put you in jail for three days, because you crossed the border illegally."

Most of these Austrian vineyards had belonged to Hungarian peasants from Szentpéterfa before the Iron Curtain went up, and I remembered that my father had spent a lot of time with these people in their wine cellars. The folks from Szentpéterfa often invited my father to grape harvests, birthday celebrations, and social gatherings because they always enjoyed an excuse to drink.

We arrived in Austria on the Feast of St. Mary. The village was preparing for a litany in honor of the Virgin Mary at a very beautiful chapel in the vineyards that lined the mountains. The family that had taken us in invited us to accompany them. We were happy to go to the church to give thanks to God for saving us and keeping us alive, and to ask for His continued help in the uncertain future. Within minutes, the news spread in the church that two Hungarian refugees had arrived and were in need of help.

The litany did not end until after ten o'clock. The old men and women of the village were standing there, ready to hug and greet us. Many of them spoke Croatian and Hungarian, so we were able to communicate. A good many of them handed us a few schillings. As we were walking down the hill, the Hungarian border as seen from the safety of Austria was a pretty sight. That is, until we noticed that in the lower part of Szentpéterfa, rockets were exploding and there was some chaotic activity. This lasted for quite a few minutes before all went silent. We knew that something was happening at the border, but we had no idea what.

We returned to the house of our hosts, where they immediately offered us more food and drink. I had never met such kind-hearted people in all my life. They poured us some of their wine, and were proud to share that they had made it themselves. They then brought us a big loaf of bread from the oven, along with some delicious smoked bacon, rolls (cracklings), and red onion.

Around midnight, we heard knocking on the door. Two police officers had come to arrest us and take us to jail for the night. Our host was on friendly terms with them and convinced them to let us stay there for the night in a real eiderdown bed, instead of making us sleep on prison benches. He explained what hurdles and dangers we had overcome to arrive there, without our parents, and that now we were essentially orphans.

The police agreed to let us stay at the farmer's house, but said they would return at six o'clock the following morning. We slept soundly that night. In the morning, our hosts re-dressed the wounds on my hands and we were ready when the officers arrived. They took us to board a bus for Güssing, about thirty miles away. There was nobody else on the bus except for the driver, the two police officers, and us. We were scared, and we were starting to feel very homesick. I began to think that maybe I should not have made such a rash decision. I wondered how my parents were faring. I was so afraid of prison. I did not know what prison was like, or what was waiting for us there. Would they torture us like they did in Hungarian prisons?

As the bus reached the next village, we saw two police officers and four young men standing at the station. Four older friends from Szentpéterfa had escaped the night before, exactly when we had seen the rockets. They had crawled across the border at night, on the lower side of the village where the border was less protected.

We rejoiced that we were together again and that they, too, had made it to the free world in one piece. They told us their tale on the drive to Güssing.

While they were creeping along near the border late at night in the dark, they unexpectedly came across a soldier, gun in hand, but quiet. They stopped, debated in Croatian, and decided that they had no choice but to jump the soldier, even though one of them might lose his life. Any one of them could be hurt, but the soldier would not be able to kill all four of them. So, when one gave the signal, they all attacked the solider. But it turned out that he was not a soldier at all . . . he was not even a flesh-and-blood man, but just a scarecrow holding a broom!

All four managed to cross the border quietly. There were no minefields on that part of the border, just a single barbed-wire fence — not like the double one we had so painfully crossed. We learned that we could have chosen an easier route for our escape. These boys were able to skip across the wire on the creek shore without any injuries. But once they reached the nearest Austrian village, they were immediately stopped by the Austrian police and thrown in the local jail. Now, we were all on our way to the big prison.

We wept on the bus as we hugged each other, tearfully singing the Hungarian song *Elindultam szép hazámból* (*I Have Left My Dear Home*). Then we sat in silence because we were all terrified of what might await us in prison. We were all aware that prisoners were tortured in Russian-controlled Hungarian prisons. We could not imagine that prisons in other countries would be any different.

We arrived in Güssing, which was a small town, but still a lot bigger than Szentpéterfa. The entrance to the prison was a huge wooden gate, and the building itself was foreboding and scary. All six of us were placed in a huge room along with several hundred criminals. Murderers, thieves, and other assorted thugs were thrown together with influential people from the political, economic and cultural spheres who were not considered dangerous felons, including those who entered the country illegally. The six of us were assigned three bunk beds. An indescribable fear emanated from us, and when the other prisoners found out that we were refugees, we received even more attention. We did not speak German, however, so they could not talk to us. We were finally left alone.

We decided that it would not be smart for all of us to be asleep at the same time, so we scheduled different sleeping times. While some of us were actually sleeping, others were just pretending to sleep, but were really on guard. We were truly afraid of these criminals. We were young, handsome men, and anything could have happened to us. We got through the night with just a few attempts to get at us that we handled easily.

In the morning, we got plain caraway seed soup for breakfast. For lunch, we got the same caraway seed soup with pieces of stale bread. For dinner? Caraway seed soup again. This would be a good diet for weight-loss, but it soon became almost torture for us. I was unable to eat caraway seed soup for many years.

At three o'clock on the third day, the officers opened the prison gate (I can still recall its squeaking sound) and said, "You are free. You can go wherever you want. The world is yours."

We were really happy to be free again, of course, but in reality we knew no one, we did not speak the language, and we had very little money. We were free, but what was going to happen to us in this big world? We looked up at the sky, and asked God what the six of us—orphaned, teenage boys—could do in a strange country without our parents.

"We need to split up into three and three," I suggested. "Three of us will walk on one side of the street, while the other three walk on the opposite side of the street. One group should speak in Croatian, the other in Hungarian, as loud as we can. Hopefully, somebody will speak to us before too long." I saw this as the best way to tell people who we were, and why we were there and the others agreed. Alfonz and I had the schillings we had received after the litany, but the others' pockets were empty.

We started to walk and my group soon came upon a tavern. The owner, a big man in a white apron, was sitting outside in the sun. When he heard us speaking Croatian, he addressed us in our language. I whistled to the others on the far side of the street. The other three joined us, and the six of us were so excited we besieged the tavern-keeper. "Calm down, calm down. Come on inside," he said. He gave us each a glass of beer, and told his wife to bring us food. We enjoyed the cold cuts she brought very much after the three-day caraway-seed soup diet in prison.

He was a very kind and decent man. He made us feel welcome, and we probably drank more than we should have. Of the six of us, I was the only one who no longer smoked; the others were puffing away like chimneys. They were also tipsy from the beer, none of them thinking of the fact that we still needed a place to sleep that night. Because I am a meticulous person and like to have everything organized, I had to act. I went to the tavern-owner and said, "Sir, we thank you very much for everything you have given us, but we will have to find a place to sleep for tonight, and after that we will need to find jobs. Where should we work, where should we go, and what should we do in our new country?"

"If you have no other option," he replied, "you can spend the night here on the floor. I will bring blankets, and we will look for something else tomorrow." I said thank you, but he continued, "Wait, I'll phone somebody."

Rotterdam Days

The tavern-owner called the owner of a sawmill about twenty miles away and said, "There are six young men here. They look like good manpower; each one has more muscle than the next." (Actually, I was not that muscular). The boss of the sawmill replied, "Good, I will send my son to fetch them. They can sleep here, and I will put them to work tomorrow."

The tavern-owner told me this fantastic news, and I both sang and cried over our good luck. I told the other boys the great news, which was followed by more spirited drinking and celebration.

An hour later, a young man of eighteen or so arrived in a beautiful Mercedes. He did not speak a word of Hungarian or Croatian. He kept speaking to us in German, which we could not understand. Still, he managed to get us in his car and off we went. I promised myself that I would not give up until I had a Mercedes just like his. Thirty-three years later, I bought my first Mercedes, and have been faithful to it ever since. I was already setting goals for myself, and even though I did not know how I was going to reach them, my determination was strong enough to push me onward.

The young man who came to pick us up sped down the road, and in no time we arrived in the village of Rotterdam (*Vörösvár* in Hungarian) where there was a big sawmill. He directed us into a large stable, gave us blankets, and told us to sleep on the haystack. The stable was pleasant enough and we slept like babies until morning.

We were woken up in the morning and brought into a small, one-room house. There were three double beds in it, one table with a bucket, but no stove or any other furnishings. It was interesting to discover that the house stood on the banks of the Pinka River, the same river that ran through Szentpéterfa. When I asked them where the toilet was, they stared at me surprised. "Where else would it be?" they said pointing to the river. I asked where we could wash our clothes, and I received the same answer: "Can't you see the river right there?" I learned that the water from the river served both the bucket and the pitcher.

A few hours later, we were taken into the office where we met the boss. He gave us work clothes, and by afternoon we were working at the sawmill. The boss was a man named Benkő—a name I remembered.

Back when my father was still working for Count Paly, one of his responsibilities was the distribution of the land and forests. I remembered that my father had given the man standing before us a parcel of forest and land, and that he had become rich from these forests. I also remembered that my father had told me that this man was heading up a sawmill and had bought plots of forest from others. In fact, this man could thank my father for this vast forest he had come to oversee.

Benkő spoke only a little broken Hungarian, but I persistently explained to him who I was, and mentioned my father's name with frequency. "Oh, yes, yes, I remember him," he finally said. "Your father is a really good man." But it did not occur to him to help us out, so we continued to work alongside the locals. He never made any kind of gesture toward me even though a little help would have been nice.

In the end, I was just happy to have a job and to be well treated. Benkő, however, was cold and tight-fisted and we never got a penny more than we earned. I was sad; I wanted him to extend the same kindness to me that my father had shown to him. It was hard, but I learned a lot from this experience, and came to understand that the world is full of less-than generous people.

They worked us really hard at the sawmill. We had to load and unload railway lines from trucks and transport very large logs from the forest to the sawmill. At first, this kind of work was really tiring, but we were hard workers. Before long the foremen realized that we were not only diligent and good workers, but that we were smart, as well.

We were all promoted to better positions. For example, I became the head of the biggest sawing machine. My job was complex. I had to supervise and control the cutting of boards from logs. I was very proud of myself because, of the many possible workers, I was the one who got this position. Not because the boss helped me, but because I deserved it. My friends were promoted to higher positions at the sawmill, too. We were able to do the kinds of work that demanded we use our heads to intelligently execute tasks.

The village where we worked was close to Szentpéterfa. All of us missed our parents terribly. We got to know the people who lived in the village, as well as the other workers. One Sunday, we decided to ask a few others to drive us to a place where we could see our village from Austria.

There, an incredible thing happened. I climbed to the top of a haystack to get a really good view of the garden at my house. It was after lunch, around two o'clock. Others had also climbed onto the haystack to look at the village with binoculars. Since we did not dare to write or call our parents, we were hoping to at least catch a glimpse of them.

As I stood staring, I suddenly spotted my father on top of the haystack next to our house. He was looking westward, towards us! It was a touching, yet heartbreaking, moment. Each of us was looking for, and found, the other. It occurred to me that God had decided that we were supposed to see each other one more time before I left for America.

We both stood there on the top of our respective haystacks, waving at each other across the border, with tears streaming down our faces. We shouted to each other as well, but unfortunately we were too far apart to hear the other's voice. We waved to each other for a long time, until our arms tired. We repeated this ritual on several Sundays, for as long as the weather allowed.

Years later, I asked my father which of us stopped climbing on the haystack first, but neither of us could remember. It warmed my heart on those Sundays when we cried for each other, all the while happy to see one another. It was an experience I kept with me, one that helped me establish another goal when I got to America: to bring my parents there, if only for a visit.

My escape partner, Alfonz Szoldatits, in Austria in 1956.

The congregation making a pilgrimage to the Shrine of Our Lady of Mariazell in 1956.

Proudly wearing the first gift I bought for myself in Austria after escaping from Hungary in 1956 – a sweater.

Hungarian refugees at the Shrine of Our Lady of Mariazell. Bottom row, left to right: Lászlo Mészáros, János Skrapits, Rudi Jurasits, János Jáni; Top row: József Zimics, Bandi Németh, Félix Jurasits, Lajos Nemeth.

Meanwhile, in Vörösvár, people came to know us and even started to befriend us. They knew that we were good workers and decent men who knew how to behave, even though we liked to let off steam. All six of us were good singers, and we often sang for them. They listened in amazement. They liked us so much that they invited us to carry the cross on a pilgrimage to the Shrine of Our Lady of Mariazell, the most visited Marian shrine in Central Europe, nestled high in the mountains of Austria. Perhaps because Our Lady of Mariazell is of Hungarian origin, the leaders of the church heard about our group and gave us this great honor. The experience of carrying the cross, praying, and singing will never be forgotten and we will be forever grateful for that opportunity.

The Dangers of Courting the Village Queen

In every village, there was a so-called "queen," the prettiest girl who everybody wanted to date. There was a "queen" in this village, and she was very beautiful indeed. Her name was Gertrud and she had her eye on me, which made me very happy because I had my eye on her as well. She invited me to her home, where we had dinner, drank beer, and enjoyed ourselves.

Our verbal communication was choppy and superficial at first because she only spoke a little Croatian or Hungarian, and I was not yet fluent in German. Luckily, eating and drinking is universal, so we did not have problems. The local boys threatened me many times, trying to persuade me to leave her alone. They envied me, but I didn't pay any attention to them. I should have, though, because a few days before I left Austria, they gave me a beating. The girl's parents wanted me to settle down with them and marry her, with the assurance that they would pass along their entire holdings and fortune. I, on the other hand, had much bigger dreams than becoming a farmer in Austria. I really liked Gertrud, but my goal was to go to America and build my future there.

I was not the only one thinking this way. All six of us applied to Catholic Charities for immigration to America. It took more than a year until the last of us—me—left Austria. We were placed on different ships, so we ended up arriving in different parts of our new country. My friend Alfonz, with whom I had crossed the border, had a relative in Toronto, Canada, not too far from Buffalo. He applied there and his relatives helped him immigrate. The rest of us had to wait until we were given an opportunity to board a vessel and head toward America. I did not know where the others had gone because I never received word from them. Why was I the last one? I did not know, but the answer became clear when I arrived.

Gertrud begged me to stay, but that possibility never crossed my mind. I could think only of America. When I was saying good-bye to her, her parents—who were crying—said, "Do not go, but if you go, please come back, because our daughter adores you." I told them that I also liked their daughter, but I still did not know what love was, and I had to take my own path, the one that I planned and envisioned for myself. I tried to convince Gertrud to join me, telling her that if she learned to speak English I would take her with me, though nothing came of it.

That final night, after saying good-bye to her and her parents, I started walking home to get a good night's sleep. My route took me through a deserted area, where there was almost no traffic. This is when the boys who had threatened me suddenly jumped out of the bushes. There were three or four of them. Two grabbed my hands, the other my legs, and they began hitting me so hard that I thought I might die. They beat my stomach, my shoulders, and my face. I screamed at them. "Beat me, you will have to stay here anyway, you will remain hicks for the rest of your lives, and nothing will come of you. Gertrud loves me."

At this they punched and kicked me more, until they finally let me go. When I left to start my journey to America the next day, every part of me was swollen, I had two black eyes, and my whole body ached. This memorable experience taught me to keep quiet when there are four against one.

FIVE | **ALL ABOARD!**

So, just like that, I left. A few days later, I was sitting on a train to Bremerhaven, a port city in Germany where I boarded the USNS General Harry Taylor (T-AP-145) on October 11, 1956. It was used to transport American soldiers to the war and this was its last trans-Atlantic trip before it was retired.

And thus began a very interesting and transformative period for me. The most painful thing about it was that I was completely alone and I was heading to an unknown place where nobody would be waiting for me. I thought about how strange that was, that I did not know anyone at my destination. All I knew was that, once I was in America, I would go to Buffalo. Where Buffalo was, what kind of place it was, what part of America it was in, who lived there, and what I was going to do there, I had no idea. I just went.

I got on the boat with just a small bag holding a few articles of clothing, some socks and underwear. I had one dollar in my pocket. I had sent the little money that I earned in Austria home to my parents. All the expenses on the ship were sponsored and paid for and, at that time, based on the stories I had heard growing up, I naively thought that when I landed in America, money would just be handed to me.

The departure was emotionally gut-wrenching. On the shore, a 120-member band began to play. I could not even believe what they had chosen to play. Here I was, all alone, not a soul by my side or on the dock to wave good-bye to me, and this incredible band played a song with the lyrics: "*Midőn Havannában hajóra szálltam én, elbúcsúzni akkor senki sem jött felém.*" (*When I boarded the ship, no one came to say good-bye to me.*) This has been my favorite song ever since.

I cried the entire time the ocean liner was at dock. Most of those on board were seen off by relatives and acquaintances; everybody was waving at each other, shouting good-bye. I was the only one standing there all alone, seventeen-years-old, waving at the world.

I picked myself up and found something promising to focus on—I was moving toward my dream. I decided to give thanks to God for letting me get this far, and I was desperately hopeful that He would stay with me for the rest of the journey. The only thing that fortified me was the fact that He had helped me get through so much already, so I knew I would be able to survive this as well.

I stood on that huge ship, knowing that in a few hours I would see only the Atlantic Ocean around me. Water everywhere, nothing else. I had no idea how far away the American continent was or when we would arrive. I later learned that it would take about eight days to get to New York.

After we left the harbor, the ship began to rock. It was not long before land disappeared from sight. My stomach began to churn and I became so seasick that I did not eat or drink for days. My bed was lodged at the bottom of the ship, part of a four-level bunk bed. I suffered on this bed the entire trip. It was so narrow that a larger man would not even have fit on it. I could not turn from my stomach to my back in that bed. I had to decide in advance in what position I wanted to sleep. If I wanted to sleep on my stomach, I had to slide in on my stomach. I could not sleep on my side because the space was just too tight.

When we went for breakfast, most of the passengers stood on the stairs spewing out their dinner from the night before. Almost everybody was seasick because of the storms we were sailing through. The weather became worse and the storms grew stronger and stronger; finally, we could not even go up on the deck anymore. Five days went by; I ate just two oranges. I lost a lot of weight.

On day six, it was announced that we would not arrive in New York in eight days as scheduled, but that the trip would take as long as twelve days because we were circumnavigating a large storm. Indeed, twelve days would pass before we docked in New York City.

There were 1,950 of us on board the ship, mostly Yugoslavians and Germans, along with a few other nationalities. As far as I knew, I was the only Hungarian. I was lucky I was able to have real conversations with the Yugoslavians because I was fluent in Croatian, and by then, I also was conversant in German. This helped alleviate my loneliness.

One evening, to keep ourselves entertained, people of many different nationalities began performing – there was dancing and singing, people playing the piano and the accordion. Passengers were sitting together in groups, tipsy, yet singing. I asked the piano player if he knew any Hungarian songs. I thought it was high time that Hungarians took a spot in the line-up of performances, as this was an international evening. Surprisingly, the piano player replied in Hungarian, "Which song should I play for you?" I was shocked! What were the chances of that?

It turned out he was Hungarian. "Well," I said, "I would like to sing *"Piros Pünkösd Napján Imádkoztam Érted"* (*I Prayed for You at the Day of Pentecost*). "I can play that," he said and began. Hungarian music is quite different from German or Slovakian music. It has an immense amount of feeling and storytelling that is beautiful and sentimental. The piano player gave me the microphone and without any warm-up, I sang this beautiful song.

This was the first time in my life that I had sung in front of a crowd that large. In Szentpéterfa, we sang a lot with friends and in groups, but for me to get up on a stage was huge. The pianist played the song very beautifully. I knew the lyrics and was confident singing it. I was worried about only one thing: that I might have to throw up mid-way through. Fortunately, my stomach cooperated.

My performance was a big success, and it appeared everybody liked it. I also got some notoriety because the pianist stood up at the end of the performance and told the audience that I was a refugee from a Communist country and asked them to accept me as their friend.

My seasickness never disappeared completely, but as we got closer to America, I began to feel better, and by the end of the voyage, both the storms and the sickness had dissipated. I had made a few friends following my performance, and when we learned we were approaching our final destination, we rejoiced together.

PART TWO

AMERICA

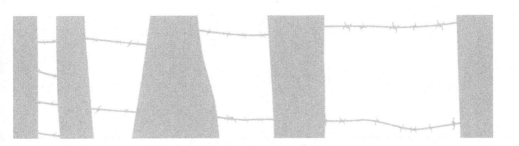

SIX | LANDING IN AMERICA

As the gigantic steamer plowed its way through the waves, more and more of us poured out onto the deck to see the fantastic sight. After twelve long days at sea, we were finally sailing past Lady Liberty. She appeared to be waiting to welcome us to the New York harbor and the United States, my new country.

Finally, an end to the endless sea, the solitude and the rolling nausea; and an end to the monstrous fear of everyday life in Communist-held Hungary. The thrill of it all caused a temporary euphoria.

When I saw the city, I was amazed. It is impossible to do justice to what I witnessed. I believe that every one of the 1,950 travelers on the ship was left just as breathless with relief as I was at the end of the dubious unknown and the dawn of this beautiful new reality. I could not imagine what a skyscraper was like until I actually saw one. I may have seen them in photos, but to stand before one of the towering giants was quite a different thing altogether.

In Hungary, we were all schooled to think of Moscow as the place to go — the most important city in the world. I knew of New York, but only what I was taught in school, and therefore, not nearly enough. I had heard talk about "the American Dream," however, and decided to put myself at risk to take a chance at finding it.

It was incredible just watching all the ships maneuver through the harbors and docks. There were huge blocks to guide the vessels, and the ships swam nicely in between them. Luckily, by 1956, the practice of stopping foreign ships at Ellis Island was no longer in place. We did not have to take physicals nor were we searched. Immigration was not as strict, and the United States no longer accepted only the healthy, turning away the sick. We were spared that potentially dehumanizing experience.

Moving at a snail's pace until there was no motion left, the ship docked. The power of that experience awed me. Then I heard my name being called over the loudspeakers, and I was summoned up to the deck.

Puzzlement was my immediate reaction. My new friends were also surprised. "Wow! Why are they asking for you? Who are you?" A thought slammed into my mind, and I shuddered. Maybe I am being called because I am in trouble. Oh my God, what did I do? Then for a moment, I thought perhaps a talent agent had been so impressed with my singing that he wanted me to sign a contract to perform in New York City.

So off I went, shaking in my shoes, to the upper deck where a group of strangers instructed me to sit under an American flag with three other men and handed me a newspaper. I was not able to read the paper that we held in front of us—it was written in English—so I had no idea what it said. Five photographers descended upon us, cameras flashing, taking multiple pictures. I was wondering about the welcome I had just received, and I could not understand. Why me?

The newspaper headlines that greeted me on October 23, 1956 when I arrived in New York City, courtesy of The Daily Mirror.

HUNGARIAN ESCAPEES here on refugee ship read of riots in homeland. From left: Imre Donsec, bound for New Brunswick, N. J.; Istran Doncsecz, heading for Youngstown, O.; Laszlo Meszaros, going to Bayside, Queens, and Otto Bogyo, settling in Cleveland. Meszaros fled into Austria through mine fields and barbed wire.

It all went so fast and I was treated gently and with kindness. Once I realized that I wasn't in trouble, I was impressed. I thought, "What a welcome to the United States!" I was happy because they had singled me out and was hoping they might give me a few bucks, but no such luck. Before I understood what was happening, the reporters had gotten up and left.

I will tell you this much for sure. It was not an accident that on my very first day in the U.S.A., I made the news!

On the front page of the newspaper, I saw photographs of mines, Molotov cocktails, dead children, and bleeding soldiers. I asked someone to read the article to me in German. That's when I found out: on that very day, October 23, 1956, the Hungarian Revolution had begun. The photos and headlines told the story, and when the media found out there was an escapee from Hungary on the ship, they came over, took pictures and published them.

I was shocked. All I could think about was my family. My father and mother were there. What about my two sisters? Oh God, what was going to happen to them? I ran to the captain. "Captain, sir! Please, you have to turn the ship around. I have to get back to Hungary right now! There is war there, and my family is all there. I have to go!" Of course, I was crying out in Hungarian. I was in agony, and the pain was doubled because I knew no one could understand me.

I begged the Captain to turn the General Taylor around, because I had to get back and fight for my country.

I was so naive that I actually thought that the ship would turn around and I could get back home in eight days. I finally got my wits about me and asked some of the passengers in German to tell the Captain that I wanted to go home. But no one really understood. It was so confusing. They were all smiling at me, telling me that the ship was not going to go anywhere anymore.

I became very sad, knowing what was going on back home just as I was arriving in America, all alone. Okay, I thought to myself, I will pack my things, just like everyone else. After I get off this thing, I will figure something out. I will find a way to get back to my family.

All of a sudden, an African-American man was coming toward me, calling my name. I had heard of black people, but I had never seen a black person before. I remembered Nénje saying, "Lacika, I have seen on TV shows just how bristly, like a brush, black people's hair is."

As the man continued to approach me, I just stared at him. How he knew me, I did not know, but he knew my name. He was very tall, at least six and a half feet. And I—being young and naive, and momentarily distracted by what was happening—climbed up on the bench next to him and started to touch his hair with my right hand. I wanted to see if Nénje was right.

The man laughed. I'm sure he had no idea why I was stroking his hair, but he let me do it anyway. Only now do I realize just how patient and compassionate he was. Truly, a good sport. As he was laughing, I saw his thick lips, and his huge, beautiful teeth. People around us were watching, uncomprehending.

It was like a scene out of a movie. I made a mental note, right then. I must write to Nénje to let her know that she was right. When I was done touching his hair, the man spoke to me in English. I did not understand a word he was saying, but I knew that he wanted me to go with him. He was kind, and since he knew my name already, I thought it must be okay. Even though I did not know where we were going, I started walking with him. I had to trust someone.

He showed me to his car. It was a New York cab, just like hundreds of other cabs. For the next several hours, he chauffeured me all around New York City—actually, the entire island of Manhattan. I later learned that he was killing time until he was scheduled to deliver me to my next destination.

We spent the whole afternoon together. At noon he bought me a sandwich, "a sub," he called it. This was the first time I had heard of a sandwich called a sub; I had no idea what it was. He also offered me a soda. He took me to see the Hudson River and was chattering on and on; I understood not one word of what he was saying, but I was in awe of the city. It was loud and huge. I had heard it was a city that never slept. I could see that now. Even the streets were wild. The traffic zoomed by, and I thought several times that we might not survive that crazy ride.

And then there were the buildings. The skyscrapers went on forever. Sometimes, I couldn't even see the tops. I kept talking to my new friend, the driver, in German, as if he could understand. The whole thing was quite interesting. My taxi driver was the kindest, friendliest, and most altruistic man I had ever met. He gave me a very good first impression of America and the American people.

Around four o'clock that afternoon, he took me to Grand Central Station. This man, whose name I never did learn, walked me to a big waiting room and talked to a conductor. He bought me a train ticket. I thought he was saying that I was to stay right there on that bench until somebody came for me. But I was guessing, and was never quite sure what he was really saying, as wave after wave of homesickness rolled over me once again.

My new friend shook my hand, said good-bye, and turned and walked away, leaving me there, sitting all alone on the bench.

By this time I was hungry again. However, I only had the one single dollar that I had brought from Austria. At the station, there was a place that sold grilled chicken. You could buy a whole chicken for ninety-nine cents. My mouth watered when I saw that they sold potatoes and rice, too, but I was not able to buy anything else, just the chicken, for ninety-nine cents. I slid the one-cent change into my pocket and, believe it or not, I still have that penny today. It serves as a great reminder of how far I've come. I finished the entire chicken right there, so I was feeling a little better.

At nine o'clock in the evening, the entire station became empty. I was sitting there, in the Grand Central Terminal of New York City, and I was wondering what I was going to do next, what was going to happen to me here? I was so lonely, and wondered, what have I gotten myself into? My mind started playing tricks on me. What am I doing here? I don't know anyone in this country. Why did I ever come here?

I dealt with the familiar nauseating fear the way I always had. I told myself, what is going to be, will be. God has helped me my entire life, I knew He was still with me. Look at what I'd already done. I was almost an adult by the time I was six. So, with God's help, I knew I would find my place somehow here, as well. I just had to wait.

Around half past nine, I heard the clicking of a woman's high heels on the tile floors of the station. It was so quiet in that lobby that you could have dropped a needle and everybody would have heard it. The high-heeled woman approached me.

"László Mészáros?" She was reading from a piece of paper in her hands. I boldly corrected her and said, "Mészáros László." She was very kind and polite, but she too, was talking to me in English. "Ja, that's me," I replied.

She put me on the train around half past ten. She spoke briefly to the conductor and then said good-bye to me. Twelve hours later, I arrived in another city in New York State: Buffalo.

SEVEN | MY NEW HOME: BUFFALO, NEW YORK

D r. Juhasz, the head of Catholic Charities, and a person who just happened to be Hungarian, met me soon after the train arrived in Buffalo. What a blessing it was to finally meet someone who spoke my native tongue. Dr. Juhasz told me all that would happen now. "László, we are going to get you a room in the Hotel Virginia for a few weeks. We'll provide you with food, someone will come and take you to buy some clothes, and soon we will find you work."

It all sounded promising, but there was still so much to deal with. After Dr. Juhasz left, I was by myself in the Hotel Virginia. I soon began to realize just what kind of place this was, this "hotel." I watched as men and women met up. I knew these meetings were secret. Sometimes you don't have to be told, you just know. Funny, though, after a while I found myself wishing that someone would come to meet up with me, too. I was so alone.

Two long weeks later, there was a knock on the door. I was hoping that one of the hotel ladies might be there. But it was the Catholic priest from Szentpéterfa standing there in my doorway. Truly, an even more welcome guest! "You probably don't remember me, but you and I are from the same village. I know your mother and father." He then told me his name: Father Skrapits. He had escaped Hungary five years earlier and now here he was.

I was crying with happiness. Someone from my very own village! Father Skrapits took me out to dinner and we had a nice talk. He explained that he found me because he went to the Catholic Charities headquarters and read the lists to look for refugees from Hungary. He always perked up when he read a name from his hometown of Szentpéterfa, and this day he found the Mészáros name and knew it had to be me.

Father Skrapits talked and talked to me, explaining what was going to happen over the next few months. He told me all about the network of volunteers from the Hungarian community in Buffalo, as well as Catholic Charities, all willing to help, all dedicated to assisting refugees from Eastern Europe trying to make a new life in America. There was also a community hall called the American-Hungarian Social Club where refugees could find support.

I owe—well actually, many of us owe—such a huge debt of gratitude to Catholic Charities. They assisted so many refugees from Hungary after World War II and the 1956 Hungarian Revolution. We are also very indebted to an anonymous Buffalo couple with no children, who donated the funds to Catholic Charities needed to bring twenty-five refugee teenagers from Hungary to the U.S. Some came to Buffalo; others went to other cities. The couple insisted on just one restriction: They did not want to meet any of the refugees. Why? They feared they might become too attached to them.

After dinner, Father took me to meet a friend of his, or so he said. We approached the apartment and knocked on the door. Suddenly, the threshold lit up with the most welcome sight I had ever seen. It was the smiling face of one of my dearest friends – Lajos (Louie) Nemeth.

Louie and I grew up in the same village in Hungary. He was one of my fellow escapees, my mentor in Austria, and remains one of my best friends to this day. When he left Austria, I had no idea where he ended up. The joy we experienced was immeasurable. Although Louie had only been in Buffalo a month and a half, he already had a job, an apartment, and had started making a new life for himself.

Just three days after Louie and I were reunited, I left the Hotel Virginia and moved into his apartment in North Tonawanda, a suburb of Buffalo. When we decided to share this place, our good times began. In fact, Louie and I got along so well that we lived together in various places right up until we each got married.

The Perils of Illiteracy

Having very little money, the apartment we shared was a bare room in a third floor attic. There was no furniture, no closets, and only a double mattress on the floor. The only heat in the apartment was an old-fashioned, cast-iron floor register, which doubled as our makeshift cook top—the only place we could warm our milk to drink with cookies.

One day, Louie came home from work very tired. Both of us were very hungry and thirsty, so we decided to go to the grocery store. This was the first time either of us had been in a big store like this. We were totally shocked to see shelf upon shelf loaded with all kinds of good stuff.

Our eyes zeroed in on a long shelf with all kinds of cookies in fancy boxes and bags, each more attractive than the next. Most of the pictures shown were of various types of dogs, one prettier than the next. We thought nothing of it and bought a gorgeous bag of "bow-tie" shaped cookies. We finished our shopping trip with a quart of milk and a six-pack of beer to round out our diet.

We could hardly wait to get home and start munching on our cookies, dunking them in milk. The cookies were delicious, and the beer quenched our thirst.

As we were enjoying ourselves, the landlady came up to collect the rent (four dollars a month), and to see if we needed anything. When she saw us munching the cookies from the bag, her eyes almost popped out of their sockets. She looked panicky, pointing to the dog on the bag. We agreed that it was a great shot of a dog, but then she started waving her hands and saying, "NO, NO, NO."

We had no idea what she was trying to tell us. We offered her a taste, but she refused, so we continued to munch. She started jumping up and down, barking like a dog "ruff, ruff," and tried to take the bag away from us. Of course, we did not let her do that. We thought she had gone totally nuts. The dog pictures seemed to have affected her badly, for some reason.

Louie and I were nervous. We needed to get her out of the room. We wanted to throw her out, but the challenge was too big. Actually, she was too big, a huge, big-boned lady. So we just sort of chased her out.

At no time did it register with us that we were eating something we shouldn't have been eating. You have to understand. In Hungary, the dogs were fed left-over food and bones, not cookies packaged in wonderful boxes.

The very next day, we got the point—and an important English lesson—when we described the previous day's incident to a fellow Hungarian. He laughed hysterically as he informed us that we were eating dog biscuits. Need I say more?

EIGHT | **WORKING IN AMERICA**

When we were reunited, Louie was working at Remington Rand in the city of Tonawanda. Catholic Charities continued to search for work for me, but at seventeen, I was under-aged and needed parental permission to work almost anywhere in Buffalo. Finally, through God's guidance and our Hungarian-American Social Club connections, Sandor Szabo, a member of the Club, found a position for me at Kraus Shingle Panel Company, where he worked. The factory was located on the East Side of Buffalo, on Cornwall Avenue, off Delevan Avenue. I would be making twenty-six dollars a week for forty hours of hard labor. It was honest work, although very dirty. I was just happy to finally have an income.

The factory was so dirty that we had to wear overalls. I would arrive at work, put on the overalls and then put all of my belongings: my clothing, my wallet, identification, immigration papers, and such, into a locker that I then closed and locked.

All day long we assembled and painted shingle panels to be used on houses. After just two weeks of employment in America, I received my first small, yellow envelope containing twenty-six dollars, cash.

That Friday morning, as usual, I locked up my clothes, all of my papers, my wallet, and for the first time, my little yellow envelope, and walked out to the warehouse to start working. There stood my trainer, leaning over the paint and turpentine buckets with a lit cigarette hanging from his mouth. I warned him again. In fact, I had been warning him off and on since I started. "Don't smoke cigarettes in here! All these liquids are very flammable!"

Sure enough, at three o'clock, just an hour before quitting time, my trainer stood over the turpentine smoking and lecturing me. This time, though, he accidently dropped the lit cigarette into the can. Immediately, the turpentine exploded into flames, and the wooden building caught fire. I will never forget the fear that swallowed me up at that moment.

On Friday, January 18, 1957, the Kraus Shingle Panel Company at 529 Cornwall Avenue in Buffalo, burned almost to the ground in just forty-five minutes! It was winter in Buffalo, a notoriously horrid time of year weather-wise, and Buffalo was living up to its reputation. It was seventeen degrees outside and there was nearly three feet of snow on the ground. It was bedlam!

Everyone was running as fast as they could away from the burning building, screaming. Everyone but me. I stayed in the building, attempting to find my way to the lockers. Everything I owned was in my locker. If I didn't get in there, I would lose the only money I had in the world, my wallet and all of my immigration and identification papers. There was no way I was going to let them go up in smoke — or so I thought.

I started toward the locker room in an attempt to recover those precious papers, but it was useless. The locker was on fire and so was more than three quarters of the building. I had to turn back, but as I did, I found that the fire wasn't only behind me, it was in front of me, too. There was only one room left. It had a steel-wire re-enforced window, nearly impossible to break through.

I smashed and smashed at it, getting bloodier and bloodier. I wrapped my arm in part of my overalls, and when the glass finally broke, the air that swept in fanned the flames even hotter.

Now I was screaming, yelling and yes, even crying. All sorts of terrible things came to mind. I thought of how my parents would be notified and how they'd feel. I asked God to save my life as He had done previously. Mostly, however, I thought about how unfair it would be if I couldn't accomplish my goals after successfully escaping to America.

As if the fire alone weren't enough of a challenge, there was almost no space to climb out into. The building next door was practically on top of the one I was in. Luckily, there was just enough room for me to shimmy out the window and squeeze through the alleyway. My first thought as I forced my way out? I thanked God that I was so skinny!

When I finally emerged out of the smoke and flames, everyone was cheering and screaming, some were even crying. They were so relieved, I later learned, because most of my fellow-workers had given up on me, sure that I was among the ashes.

They picked me up and paraded me around! Everyone was in heaven — including me. But soon, reality hit. All of my papers had burned; the only money I had earned here in the U.S. had gone up in smoke. Now I am in real trouble, I thought. But at least I was alive!

It was at that moment Sandor Szabo came to my rescue. He offered me his coat and took me to his home and he and his wife fed me a wonderful meal. Sandor gave me some fresh clothes and took me back to my apartment with Louie. I would learn that everything I lost was replaceable. This was not like the war-torn country from which I had just escaped.

Never Give Up!

Without my papers, I had no proof that I was a legal immigrant. I spent the next several months working with translators and a very kind judge, all referred to me by Catholic Charities and my fellow Hungarians, to replace my green card and working papers. If not for my social network at Catholic Charities and the American-Hungarian Social Club, who knows where I would be today. Deported, perhaps? I was on my knees daily praying until those papers came through.

Fortunately, I was still able to find work. And I had prayer, the American-Hungarian Social Club, and our close-knit community to thank for that. At that time, there was a Sheriff in Buffalo who was of Hungarian descent. This wonderful man happened to have a brother in the car business. Not just some small potatoes shop, his brother owned a car dealership on Delaware Avenue in Buffalo near Kenmore, one of the busiest streets in town.

I soon found myself washing cars, changing batteries, cleaning — anything that needed to be done for the repair shop and the showroom. It was menial work in some people's eyes, but to me it was yet another opportunity. I was pretty sneaky, too. I went in early and started learning to drive using the cars in the parking lot. This was so exciting. After all, no one in Hungary had a drivers license except the wealthy and bus drivers. Most of those in my Hungarian village commuted on foot or rode bicycles.

At first, I experimented in the parking lot. But soon I started feeling more sure of myself. One morning I purposely went into work at 6 a.m., earlier than anyone, and in a burst of bravery, I got behind the wheel of a car and ventured out onto Delaware Avenue. I was a bit anxious, but I was confident that I could get back in one piece with no unwanted incidents. I did well, and the ensuing burst of confidence stayed with me for a very long time.

I learned how to drive quickly, but then I had to tell my boss what I had been up to . . . without a license. Andy Tutuska got mad. I mean really mad! Luckily, still new to America, I only understood a few of the choice words that he used on me.

Later that week, when Andy called me into his office, you could have knocked me over with a feather when he said, "I should be firing you, but I am not."

"You aren't?"

"Les, not only am I impressed with your new skill and your excellent work ethic, but I want you to start driving cars for us—once you have a license. Let me see what I can do about that."

Two weeks later, I had a valid driver's license, and I was jumping up and down with excitement! I went straight to the Hungarian-American Social Club to brag about my new job and my new license. I even wrote a letter to my parents telling them that I had a "chauffer" certificate. Life was good. All my hard work and devilish risk-taking had paid off.

Not only had I gotten my driver's license and a promotion, but soon, at only eighteen years of age, I was able to save up a bit of money, send some home to my parents, and buy a used Pontiac with Louie and his brother, Frank. Three owners, one driver, and three separate work places. Guess what I was doing all the time?

By this time, I was beginning to realize just how much I love a challenge, and how much I wanted to learn. I could hardly sit still because I was so anxious to move forward in my life. Having conquered the challenges at the car dealership, I knew it was time to move on.

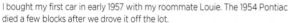
I bought my first car in early 1957 with my roommate Louie. The 1954 Pontiac died a few blocks after we drove it off the lot.

Yet Another Brush with Death

I heard there were jobs available at Bethlehem Steel, so I applied and was hired to work there at the end of 1957. I worked the swing shift, which took some getting used to. My job was to guide the crane operator in moving the H-beams onto a neat stack. I also guided the beams as the crane swung them over to my area. Those beams were huge chunks of metal, thirty feet long. I would climb up to the top of the pile and wait for the next beam to approach. Then, lining the H-beam up perfectly on the stack, I would unhook the chains that held the H-beam in place and signal the crane operator to bring another beam.

It was Christmas night, and I was on duty, helping with H-steel transport preparation. While I was at the far end of the stack completing the task, the crane operator was in the middle of his holiday celebration, drinking like a fish while he worked. I kept yelling, "Stop! Stop!" but he kept right on drinking.

I was balancing on the wooden spacers between H-beams, waiting for the crane to get into position. I saw the crane operator take another swig as he swung the crane my way. I was now screaming bloody murder. I knew he could hear me, but he ignored me completely.

I had no choice. I had to jump off the stack that was already more than seven feet high. But, it was jump or be killed. The H-beam was headed right for my skull. Just as I jumped, the H-beam caught the brim of my safety helmet, knocking it clear off my head. I landed hard on the pavement below and heard a crunch. I had broken my ankle.

I was taken to the hospital where a cast was put on my ankle. They let me go home, but I had to take off work to heal the broken bone. About eight weeks into my recovery, there was a massive layoff at Bethlehem Steel. Guess who lost his job?

During the down times between jobs, I had plenty of time to think about all I had done. It was overwhelming at times. I had arrived alone and had to learn a whole new language and a whole new culture. I had never heard or seen a football game, a hockey game, or even a baseball game. I had never eaten a banana, an orange, or any of the tropical fruits that all Americans grow up eating. Steak, lobster tails, and other more expensive foods never even crossed my path.

I learned about football—even though I hated it initially—because I had to assimilate into the culture, and sports were the social talk every day at work. This country was far different from what I knew, but I knew I needed to learn the culture to survive.

Growing Your Dreams

At that point, I was unemployed and not at all happy about it. I was certain that I would find something soon, though. One afternoon in 1958, I ran into a friend who introduced me to a painting contractor named Jack Farkas, of Hungarian descent.

My first painting job was on Colvin Avenue in Buffalo in 1959.

Jack's company did quite a bit of work in the very prestigious Middlesex Street area and along Colvin Avenue in Buffalo. In fact, there are few houses there that I didn't paint—either inside or out. I was proud of the work I did, and of the fact that I had now added yet another skill to my palette. I watched how Jack ran his business, and once again, I thought of all the ways I could do the same thing, maybe even better. I just needed the funds to underwrite my own business. My dream to become an entrepreneur was growing stronger every day.

Louie's brother, Frank, joined us the following year in America and moved into our apartment. In our residence, we had rules that we all had to obey. I was the cook, Louie was the dishwasher, and Frank cleaned up after us. In spite of all this, we had frequent visitors in our apartment—mice and rats.

One night while I was sleeping deeply, a visitor arrived. I felt someone tickling me all over my body. I started waking up, expecting a gorgeous woman to be there by my side, when all of a sudden I realized that there was a big, fat rat climbing inside my pajamas searching for food. I jumped out of bed, screaming!

Louie and Frank ran over to my room. "What's up? What's up?"

I shouted, "A big, damn rat was in my bed and now it's running around the living room. Frank, who was petrified, was of little help. So Louie and I grabbed pillows and started chasing it until we finally crushed it.

Good job! We congratulated each other, had a drink, changed the linens, and went back to bed. The visitors kept coming back until the landlord finally got rid of them.

We worked hard during the day and enjoyed ourselves in the evening. We all shared a desire to improve our lives. We attended night school together at Riverside High School to learn English, and we practiced what we were learning on our boss every day. Jack, being Hungarian, was eager to help. At times, he was more than amused, but he was happy to lend a hand—as long as it didn't interfere with our work.

Sadly, toward the end of 1958, Buffalo's economy began to suffer and painting jobs became more and more scarce. Jack didn't have the usual busy schedule for us. But I was hungry—eager to earn, eager to get ahead. I was proud, too. After all, I now had a profession, and I was damned good at it. So, Frank and I decided to go to New York City where we had heard there were jobs to be had. After all, New York City was huge. There had to be work there for two really talented house painters.

We relocated to the other side of New York State in early 1959, to an apartment in Harlem with friends. We had many Hungarian friends in the city, most of them escapees from Szentpéterfa who had arrived after the 1956 revolution. I looked for work, and quickly got a job as a painter! I was paid two dollars and twenty-five cents per hour, a modest sum in those days. My first assignment was on 74th Street painting skyscrapers. Although I did great work, I was about to have a nasty encounter with an inner demon: my intense fear of heights.

These jobs involved extreme risk, working on the outside of gigantic, tall buildings, scraping old paint and preparing window frames to be repainted. It was one thing to stand on a stepladder working on a house on Middlesex Avenue in Buffalo, but it was an entirely different thing to work in a small cage, dangling from the fifty-fourth floor of a skyscraper on 74th Street.

I had a major problem the minute I looked down. I could see nothing but cars, and they were tiny, like miniature bugs. I was shaking. I wanted to quit. I was afraid for my life. I could paint, but first the old paint had to be scraped off. It was the worst job ever because I had to use a torch. At that height, windy was the name of the game. Sparks from the torch and the burned off bits of paint were always blowing all over the place. My hands, face, and clothing were covered with burns.

At fifty-four stories above the ground, the only concern is not falling, so you don't dare jump out of the way of the burning embers. You just suffer through it. The fear was awful, but I told myself: Never give up! It's just another obstacle in your life. So I stayed . . . for a while.

Because I was determined, I advanced. From the fifty-fourth floor to the fifty-seventh floor, and also financially, because I was working ten to twelve hours a day.

I must admit, however, that even I have my limits. I will never forget the tipping point.

The apartment I was sharing was in Harlem, a notoriously poor area where mice, rats and cockroaches were frequent visitors. One evening, exhausted after a hard day at work, I decided to take a hot bath in the metal tub in the middle of the kitchen. After filling the tub with water, I settled in for a soak, quickly nodding off to sleep. I thought I was dreaming, but I suddenly awoke to a tickling feeling all over. When I finally opened my eyes, my entire body was covered with cockroaches, hundreds of cockroaches. I started screaming and jumped out of the tub, doing everything I could to kill every last one of those damned bugs.

Here is a true confession: New York was the "Big City," but Buffalo was more to my taste. Very soon after this, on New Year's Eve, only eight months after we left Buffalo, both Frank and I returned to our first "adopted home," to pursue our careers. Truth be told, there was also a girl there whom I had left behind and whom I would later marry.

The roommates—like brothers. With Louie and Frank by my side.

I was out of work sporadically, but never for too long. I'm very proud to say I have never collected unemployment benefits. I found small jobs here and there, enough to buy essentials for the kitchen. There were weeks when I had next to nothing, but I was always looking. In Hungary, there was no such thing as unemployment benefits, so it never seemed like an option.

Shortly after I returned to Buffalo in 1960, I landed a job as a laborer in another factory, J.H. Williams on Wolcott Street. I was working for a tool manufacturer, mostly sweeping and doing other menial tasks, but I was quickly promoted to the position of hammer operator. This was my very first good-paying job—$125 a week!

It was also my first real exposure to factory culture and "factory language." It really screwed up my English. I also learned the dynamics of Labor Unions. I hadn't worked at Bethlehem Steel, another unionized company, long enough to gain a full appreciation of that world.

On payday, every Friday, my co-workers and I would head right for the bar. Most of them drank their paycheck, but I just had a beer or two, and that was it. I can recall a number of stories about socializing with my colleagues at J.H. Williams, many of them very funny, but there is one that really stands out.

I was introduced to a new game that I will never forget. A worm, a shot, and a beer were the goals—and I do mean a real worm. You had to show you were a man, I guess, and swallow a worm, whole, then chase it with a shot of whiskey. It was a contest, to see who could do more. If you didn't participate, you became an outcast, kicked out of the group. I wanted to be a part of the team, so I tried! I got that gooey, squirming worm about halfway down, and all of a sudden, I pulled it back out. I ran to the men's room and, you can guess what I did there. That was the first and last time I ever tried to swallow a worm. I tried it, therefore, I was allowed to remain in the group. Great mentality, right?

That might have been the critical moment when I decided I wasn't happy at J.H. Williams, but it wasn't. The really pivotal moment came later.

I was having lunch with my colleagues, admiring one of the lunch boxes, and thinking I should have one myself. When the owner of the box told me that he was proud of it and had been carrying it, day-in and day-out, to work for forty years, I froze. In fact, I didn't sleep for the next few nights. I could not foresee myself staying at that job for the following forty weeks, let alone forty years. I trembled at the very thought. I knew then that I was a person who needed variety and the opportunity to advance. I needed a career.

I have a great deal of admiration for people who work on the factory floor, but I did not come to this country—this "land of dreams"—to work as a laborer all my life. My "lunchbox lesson" prompted me to start looking aggressively for another job. There were too many opportunities available in life. I made the decision to forfeit the security of a union job in a factory while I worked to find my future.

I felt very strongly that I was born to make a positive difference, to contribute, and to share my gifts to help other people in their lives in a major way. My father left me with a simple message: "Be honest, always do your best, take care of your family, treat people with respect, be a good citizen and follow your dream. Remember, Laci, my son, it's always better to give than to receive."

More than thirty thousand immigrants came to the U.S. after the 1956 Hungarian Revolution, in addition to the tens of thousands who came following World War II. These people brought innovative ideas and an entrepreneurial spirit, and they filled many jobs for which there was a shortage, thereby helping the U.S. economy. Most of my friends worked in factories for the next thirty or forty years. I did not. Not that I am better; I am just different. I wanted more out of life than doing the same thing, performing the same routine, day after day after day. I took a tremendous risk, jumping that fence to freedom, and, for me, it made all the difference.

NINE | EARLY SOCIAL LIFE IN BUFFALO

Like many other refugees, I was often confused. Sometimes I wondered, who am I? A Hungarian or an American? The United States was grand and rich and amazing, just as I had been told, but it was strange and odd, too. In Hungary, although I feared for my life and the lives of my loved ones, at least I understood the language; I could read the labels at the store, I knew the streets, the neighboring towns, and the customs. The dichotomy frequently sent me into a tailspin of homesickness.

My friends were so very important in my adjustment to this new country, to my new life. Were it not for the dear friends from my homeland—who had traveled to America before me, with me, or after me—and my new friends here in the United States, I am not sure how my life would have turned out. Time and time again, out of the blue, I would suddenly realize that I was on foreign shores. There was a painful jolt that accompanied each time the reality of my life surfaced. On the other hand, I was also delighted, because here is where I decided I would become a star. Truth be told, I have been known to brag a time or two and to be a bit of a ham. The constant saving grace was my circle of friends. They have kept me sane.

Upon my arrival in Buffalo on October 23, 1956, I started my life over again. I was homesick, exhausted and a bit insecure about who I was. I was seventeen and I had lived through many difficulties and challenges already. On the one hand, I had a boatload of traumatic memories from my youth, had fallen in with a rough gang as a teen, and then risked life and limb to run away and escape from a Communist-ruled country.

And yet, there was this invincible part of me that arose sometimes as just a whisper, declaring that I was destined for success. This was the part of me recognized by the press, even on the very day that I arrived in America. I felt it. I was destined to become "somebody." Especially when the cameras of the

New York City newspapers flashed like Fourth of July fireworks in my face and announced: "Laszlo Meszaros is here!"

In Buffalo, there was an American-Hungarian Social Club on Tonawanda Street in Riverside, on the west side of the city. It was started in the 1920s to find shelter for homeless immigrants. Then it evolved into a family away from family for those immigrants who were separated from their blood-relatives in Hungary. Finally, it became a center for friendship.

Shortly after I moved in with Louie, we went to that American-Hungarian Social Club. After a long and cheerful introduction, we met Hungarians of all ages who welcomed us to "America." It was an exhausting evening, but very useful and educational. We met doctors, laborers, small business owners—all kinds of people.

Everybody was interested in the story of how we managed to escape Hungary, live for nearly a full year in Austria, and then, somehow, wind up in Buffalo. We had a few beers and kept answering questions. Within a very short time, we had developed several friendships, which helped us to assimilate into this culture.

Soon we found out that there were a number of Hungarian organizations in Buffalo, and around five or six thousand Hungarian immigrants. I was very surprised that this many of my fellow countrymen were living here. There were also quite a few Hungarians living on the Canadian side of the border.

Three Different Hungarian Groups

By 1956, Buffalo was host to three distinct types of Hungarians.

First, there were those who we called the "Old Hungarian-Americans." They were part of a wave of immigration after World War I. They emigrated from Hungary in the 1920s and 1930s looking for jobs and opportunities. They were able to walk out of the country openly to seek a better life. This group was well off for the most part and had not experienced hunger or thirst in the same way the refugees did.

Secondly, there was the so-called *"Dépé,"* or D.P. (Displaced Persons) group, who emigrated after World War II, escaping the Russian-Communist horde. To this group we can add people like me, who escaped during the communist regime and within a few years arrived in America. This was more of a political group, pushed out of Hungary by the government for political reasons. In this D.P. group, there were officers, patricians, businessmen, doctors—mostly professionals.

Hungarian Organizations in Buffalo

- *AMOSZ* – Association of Hungarian-Americans
- Action Hungarica
- *A Magyar Szabadságharcos Szövetség* – The Hungarian Association of Freedom Fighters.
- *A Magyar Harcosok Bajtársi Közössége MHBK* – The Hungarian Fellow-Soldier Polity (Government Controlled Group) for elite soldiers and high ranking officers in the Hungarian Army.
- *A Magyar Csendőrök Országos Egyesülete* – The Hungarian Association of Gendarme (Special Forces).
- *Magyar Ház* – American Social Club, established during the 1930s featuring the Hungarian soccer team sponsored by the Social Club.

The main difference between the Old Hungarian-Americans and the D.P. was that the former emigrated in hope of financial gain and a better future, while the latter escaped from tyranny.

The third group, the Fifty-Sixers, was almost a branch of the D.P.s consisting of individuals who escaped after the revolution of 1956. For many, this was an opportunity to run away from the "system." Many were running from execution, prison time, or being sent to Siberia. All kinds of people belonged to this group: peasants, students, teachers, soldiers, doctors, artists, writers, young and old, humble and brave, rich and poor. The majority came by plane; they did not suffer the turbulent ocean voyage like I did.

There was little consensus among the three groups. Hungarians typically like to be right. This means that we don't always stick together.

By the time I arrived, the Old Hungarian-American group had grown older and, because of their higher status, they had very little in common with my friends and me. There was an unmistakable level of discomfort between this group and the other two. However, all three groups belonged to many of the same American-Hungarian organizations.

Groups and churches welcomed the younger generation, like me. There were Catholic, Protestant, and Lutheran churches, and one synagogue.

When I was nineteen, I helped with the Hungarian Boy Scout troop, which was sponsored by Calasanctius, a Piarist high school in Buffalo. The school enrolled only elite students with IQs over 130. The teachers and priests were from Hungary, but students of any nationality and from any school could attend. Years later, I taught Cobal (a computer language) part-time at Calasanctius. Another Hungarian revolutionary and my dear friend, Gene Hegedus, was sponsored by Calasanctius. He taught math and later became assistant principal and disciplinarian.

We young adults felt like we did not have a place of our own, though. We were too old to be Boy Scouts. Some of us became Scout leaders, but we were too young to feel comfortable with the elders at the American-Hungarian Social Club.

We tried to fit in, making appearances at the events we were invited to by these various organizations. Some had parents who took them and their friends to the special club dates. However, some of us had no living relatives here. Some of our parents were no longer alive, or were trapped in Hungary, forbidden to leave, like my parents. There was a need for a new organization, a group or community that we young newcomers could enjoy.

The Hungarian Youth Club

In 1959, we established the "Hungarian Youth Club" at the corner of Hertel and East Avenue in the Riverside neighborhood of Buffalo. We rented a property with a first floor and a basement.

Only Hungarians living in the area who had arrived a while back or right after the revolution could join this group. However, members were allowed to bring non-Hungarian boyfriends or girlfriends with us to the club and to club events. No one was excluded from the group because of money, race, or their family background; everybody was accepted. However, because the group was mixed, initially it was difficult to maintain harmony, but we managed and became united.

The establishing committee consisted of the founder, Father John (János) Skrapits, Hungarian pastor; Alex Molnár, artist and experienced theatrical actor; and Laszlo Mészáros, co-founder and president. Even though I was the youngest member, I experienced my first taste of leadership when I was elected president of the club. I was good at it, too. I helped create the operating budget and raised money from theatre productions we held. My self-esteem was in recovery, as a little shining star emerged, priming the pump for what was to happen later in my career.

The Hungarian Youth Club became quite a cultural center. Our goals were to promote pride in our Hungarian heritage, improve our knowledge of Hungary, and create a forum for young Hungarians in the area to perform plays, read poetry, and hold dances. The theatrical works, under the direction of Alex Molnár, were quite sophisticated, and were presented in Hungarian to crowds as large as three hundred. In addition to the American-Hungarian Social Club, we also presented these plays at Bannot Hall on Tonawanda Street and traveled to other locations, such as Welland, Ontario, in Canada and Niagara Falls and Rochester in New York. I am proud to say that I played the lead in many of the productions, and when we traveled, we always checked out any local Hungarian restaurants.

I remember attending dinner dances at the German, Italian, Polish, and Croatian Clubs in the area, where we did ballroom dancing. Our Hungarian dance group had about thirty participants. We learned the traditional Hungarian folk dances which we performed on Hungarian holidays, like March 15th, commemorating the Civil Freedom War in 1948; August 20th, Saint Steven's Day; and October 23rd, the start of the Hungarian Revolution.

Performing as Hungarian folk dancers in 1960. I am fourth from the left in the top row; Frank Nemeth is first from the left in the bottom row.

And that's me doing a solo.

On stage with Kathy Nádasy at the Hungarian House in 1960.

Hanging out with the guys at the beach on a Sunday afternoon. From left to right: Tibi, Louie and Frank Nemeth, John Kapitany, me, and Kornel Teleki.

We also read books about Hungarian history, American history and culture, and other literature. We talked about our careers and who was going on to higher education, and we told interesting stories from our everyday lives. We held "opera nights," listening to records in the club. We played cards and put pool and ping-pong tables in the basement, and these soon became our favorite pastimes. I was not number one in ping-pong; Tivadar (Ted), who would become my brother-in-law, was the reigning ping-pong king.

On Saturdays in the summer, whoever wasn't working went to the beach. We frequented the beaches at Beaver Island, Grand Island and at Sherkston, Ontario. We all loved the water. Swimming was a challenge and great exercise; row boating was a luxury. We couldn't even think about motorboats; those were out of our league. I still swim to this day for exercise and am proud to say that eventually, many years later, I was able to own a motorboat and take my family out on the Niagara River and Lake Erie.

On Sunday mornings, some of us went to St. Elizabeth's Hungarian Catholic Church, where several of us sang in the choir. After church, we enjoyed outdoor activities when the weather permitted. I remember wonderful picnics at Letchworth State Park. We laughed and ate great picnic foods, rode our bikes, played soccer, and chased the girls around in the woods to see if we could catch them and give them a kiss.

We also poured our hearts out and sang Hungarian songs with gypsy bands at different events. This was and still is one of my passions. Even today, when I am in Hungary and run into a gypsy band, they recognize my face, know that I love gypsy music and invite me to sing with them. These are very emotional experiences for me, very nostalgic. With themes of devotion to our mothers and fathers, and vows of love to friends and lovers, the lyrics and melodies are so beautiful.

The Youth and Social Clubs became second homes for us. Were we still homesick? Yes, but we kept it to ourselves. The songs we sang brought all that out of us, and singing those songs was a good way to forget the loneliness and sorrow in our hearts. Romantic relationships formed and dating began within the group, which also helped to ease the pain.

During this time, I was fortunate enough to meet Kathy Havas. We were good friends for many years, and her family took a great liking to me. I became a frequent visitor at their home on Sundays and holidays. I eventually

I married Kathy Havas in 1962. The Havas family became my family in America.

built up enough courage to present her with an engagement ring. Several years later, in 1962, when I was twenty-three and Kathy was twenty-one, we were married.

The Havas Family

With grace and appreciation, Kathy describes her mother and father:

"Although they lost everything during the war—their home, their country, their way of life, their friends—and left behind their families, they *never* lost their faith in God, nor their morals, nor their belief in the goodness of humankind. They were resolute, did not wallow in their losses; instead, they made a conscious choice to be happy, and assimilated into life in America.

"My father was the epitome of a gentleman. He was highly respected, intelligent, brave, wise, kind, compassionate, courteous, and fair in all his interactions, honest, patient, and he loved us, his daughters, openly and dearly.

"My mother was exuberant, warm-hearted, outgoing, hard-working, loving, nurturing, fun, and had amazing strength and determination. She too was brave and wise, and she had a radiant, beaming smile, which warmed the hearts of everyone. She always made everyone feel special."

– Kathy Havas

As Kathy explains, "We met at the Hungarian House in December of 1956, just a few weeks before my sixteenth birthday. Bogar Juci and I went there to play ping-pong, and you and Lajos were there. After the game, my friend gave us a ride in her car. In the car, you and Lajos sang Hungarian ballads and folk songs, and I totally and utterly flipped over your voice. I remember that explicitly, but the details of how we actually started dating elude me. Most of the time Lajos, then his brother Feri (Frank) and Tibi (Tivadar), and Kornel, and Jancsi came along wherever we went. Daddy used to call the lot of you 'my harem.'"

Kathy, who was Hungarian-American, was only ten years old when her family immigrated to the U.S.A. "I cannot emphasize enough just how desperately sad life was for us during those horrifying days in Hungary."

Kathy's family was not unlike many of our Hungarian families. Regardless of what we did in public, we Hungarians, like many other nationalities in Europe at the time, were a wounded community. So many had endured hardship and starvation, especially those who stayed behind. I believe that those of us who came to America were, for the most part, the lucky ones.

I loved Kathy's family very much and they always treated me as one of their own. Kathy and I had many great adventures over the years. In 1963, we ventured out and went on a cross-country trip for six weeks. I wanted to see this country before I went home and visited Budapest. In my sixteen years in Hungary, I had never had the opportunity to travel to Budapest. We ended up taking the northern route going west and returned through the middle states. The richness and the scenery overwhelmed me. The beauty of my new country was out of this world and I will never forget this trip across America.

If only to show you just what a good sport I am, I am willing to put in print some of the memories that Kathy shared from those days. After all, if you can't laugh at yourself...

"One Sunday afternoon we (you, Lajos, and I) rented a small motor boat on the Niagara River," recalls Kathy. "I asked if you knew how to operate the motor, and you, being the 'macho he-man,' said, of course. Lajos was skeptical and I was downright nervous, but I didn't want to 'show you up.' However, after you rather chaotically backed us into the dock, I had to show you how to shift the gears and handle the motor. I had learned how to handle motorboats from Lee Fisher during several years of vacationing up at Rest Island in Georgian Bay."

"Another humorous event was when we were vacationing in the Muskokas. You and Lajos were trying to fish (I say trying because you were not catching anything), while I was lounging in the sun on the bow of the boat. An older, bald, rather heavy-set man pulled up in another boat and anchored near us, dropped his line in the water, and

Fishing at Muskoka Lake with Tibi and Louie.

caught one fish after the other. Totally annoyed and baffled, you commented in Hungarian, 'It would be nice to know how that old bald, paunchy guy does it.' The man responded in Hungarian. The look of utter disbelief and embarrassment on your face was priceless. I don't remember how you talked your way out of that because I was both laughing and mortified, and rolled off the boat into the water."

Sadly, all these fun times for Kathy and I existed simultaneously with troubled times. Kathy and I appeared to be a model couple in public, but there was disharmony at home. Although Kathy had been my dream girl, and I courted her for years before the marriage took place, I was not aware that she and I had a major difference in our expectations of family life. She did not know that I wanted to have a family, above all else. This was a huge shock to us both, and as time went by, I realized more and more just how much it meant to me to have children.

Being at odds with our vision for our future created an ever-increasing friction between us, and soon the relationship was disintegrating. We kept up appearances in public, but after a decade, Kathy and I decided to go our separate ways. Our divorce was granted after one full year of Legal Separation. Kathy and me and our families continue to remain friends to this day.

During these troubled times, rather than going out with friends, drinking and having fun every night, I instead invested my energy in something positive which paid off later in life. For the duration of the marriage, I busied myself with getting my GED (high school equivalency certificate) at night school. Then I started taking college classes at night.

In addition to my marriage coming to an end, as the days, months, and years went by, one by one, we began to split away from our Hungarian Youth Club. We started to assimilate, landed jobs further away, and many of us found our partners and married. Our short-lived club slowly disbanded and finally closed in the late 1960s.

However, the friendships and relationships that started in the Hungarian Youth Club have remained strong for more than fifty years. These friendships have allowed us to grow up together and to rekindle our memories of the past. Unfortunately, many friends have passed away over the years, including Frank who was taken from this earth on July 12, 2015. I was devastated and so very sorry to see Frank go. In my eyes, he was way too young and will be missed.

We all enjoyed our free time, but we never forgot the fact that we had to make a living and fulfill our responsibilities to our employers. Work was our first priority and like many others, I give a lot of credit to the Hungarian Youth Club and the American-Hungarian Social Club for not only providing me with forever friendships, but also for my rapid career advancement.

There is no underestimating the transformative value of the support I received from this group. I will be forever grateful for the rebuilding of my self-esteem fostered by these Hungarian patriots. I was able to form a family, become grounded, and gain the courage and self-confidence that I needed to take gigantic risks in my career.

The Mushroom Story

Every summer, my friends and I would all rent cabins at Muskoka Lake, in Canada just north of Toronto. As many as twenty of us routinely spent two-week vacations in this beautiful place. We had a ball at Muskoka, fishing, drinking, swimming, drinking, and boating. Many of us loved biking, drinking, hiking, and running. Oh, and we always enjoyed drinking, or have I mentioned that? When a full crew was there, plenty of arguments or, as I prefer to consider them, vehement discussions, could be heard.

During the summer of 1972, my parents came from Hungary for a two-month visit. It was the second visit for my father, but the very first visit time my mother had come to America. It was our good fortune, or perhaps our bad luck (you decide), that the summer trip to Muskoka fell during those two months. So, off we went: Mom, Dad, my sister, her husband—about sixteen of us.

My mother suffered from a chronic illness and required a vegetarian diet. One of her favorite meals was mushrooms and Mom prided herself on knowing every type and kind of mushroom. When we were growing up, we were always out in the forest picking mushrooms, so Mom was a self-proclaimed mushroom expert.

Mom wanted to contribute. She commandeered Ildi and I to accom-

Greeting my parents at the airport on their first visit together to the U.S.

pany her to a nearby forested area where we spent hours filling basket after basket with mushrooms.

There was a lot of activity as everyone bustled around setting up for the party. Mom was excited. She made a special breading with the secret spices she had brought from Hungary and then deep-fried the mushrooms as the main course for the evening meal. We sat down to eat at 5 o'clock.

Playing cards during my dad's visit to the U.S.. From left to right: Father John Skrapits, my father, Bela Cako, and his son Csaba.

My father during his visit to the U.S.. From left to right: Dad, Gabor Papp, and me.

And what a hit it was! You should have heard the comments. "Delicious!" "Wow! What a treat!" "These are the best mushrooms I have ever eaten!" There was so much commotion; the compliments were flying. Suddenly, in the midst of the hubbub, before I even had a chance to sit down and eat, I noticed my father talking crazy, acting really bizarre.

I looked over at my sister Ildi, only to find that she was trembling, shaking like a leaf.

All of a sudden, the party was turning into a screaming nightmare. One by one, everyone was getting crazy. Even the children started screaming and carrying on.

I'm not sure what prompted this, but I gave Ildi a shot of Scotch to calm her trembling, and in seconds she started to vomit. It was clear, I had to get every one of us to the hospital. Something was going dreadfully wrong.

Our campsite was part of a larger campground, and our neighbors were staring at us. I asked them for help, and they loaded us all in their cars and got us to the closest emergency room, fast!

As the undeclared leader, I explained the scene that afternoon to the attending nurse. In seconds, she had it figured out. "Did you folks eat any mushrooms today? My guess is they were poisonous!" She calmed our fears, explaining that we would all be okay. Then she gave me enough bottles of medicine to clean us all out, and off we went, back to the campsite.

Our lovely campsite had just one restroom and twenty-two people who would need it on an emergency basis! This would take some powerful organizing. I set up groups and staggered the doses of medicine in the hope that there would be enough time in between bathroom trips to be safe. I assigned the one and only bathroom to the ladies; the guys had to use the river.

It was almost comical. My mother, for some unexplained reason, had not experienced the effects of the mushrooms. But every one of the twenty-one remaining campers were all preparing to run when the medicine hit, but not one of us had any reaction at all—nothing! All that preparation and hysteria for nothing. Within the next three to four hours, everyone had recovered and the camp was happy again.

The next morning my mother, with her great sense of humor, announced, "Lacika, let's go pick mushrooms now that I know what not to pick!"

The crowd roared a definite, "No!" and we all laughed.

PART THREE

MY PROFESSIONAL JOURNEY

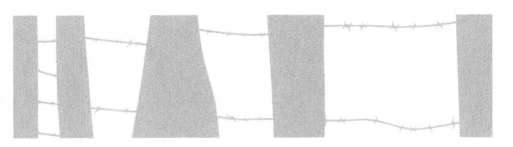

TEN | **THE ROSWELL PARK YEARS**

Late in 1960, the lunchbox experience at J.H. Williams inspired me to search for a different type of employment. I started my quest by reaching out to the people from my homeland—the network at the American-Hungarian Social Club.

As luck would have it, one of the older members, Bella Szakacs, became a good friend to all of the younger adults. He worked with us, taught us, and set a very good example for us. Bella was employed at Roswell Park Cancer Institute, working with experimental animals—injecting them, giving them drugs, performing surgery on them, and so on.

Bella said, "Let me look around at Roswell to see if I can find you a job as an animal caretaker or something. At least at Roswell there will be opportunities for you to advance. We work with the smaller-sized animals, from monkeys to mice, not cows or horses . . . just small test animals."

He called me in no time. "Les, I have a job for you. But be prepared, it only pays twenty-six dollars a week."

I showed up for my interview. Bella pointed me to a door on the left as he disappeared behind a door in the other direction. I walked into a huge room filled with dogs, mice, monkeys, cats, rats, and guinea pigs in cages. The smell? I can't even describe how bad it was. I gagged and nearly vomited. As I regrouped, I moved on to the next door.

It was Bella's lab. I looked in, and what I saw made me throw up. Ten rats were lined up on a long table. They were anesthetized and cut open.

Bella was standing there, sandwich in hand. "Les, how are you doing so far? You can watch if you want, while I inject the drugs that we are testing on these animals." He raised his sandwich. "Bon appétit."

I went home and thought very hard about whether I could even stand to go back to that lab for a minute, much less take the job. I doubted I could ever be so callous as to eat lunch while dissecting tiny animals. So for two weeks I kept my job at J.H. Williams making $125 a week, but I was miserable.

I had not one moment of peace, the decision taunting me, playing tug-of-war in my mind. The agony of what I saw in the lab and the financial risk versus the advancement possibilities at Roswell, coupled with the fact that there was no union at Roswell—what should I do? I feared that I had to risk Roswell or remain a laborer for the next forty years. But I had a dream. I wanted to be a success. And therein lay the answer to my dilemma. It was time to leave J. H. Williams for Roswell Park Cancer Institute. I said yes to Bella.

Although I left the security of operating heavy equipment at J. H. Williams for the relative lack of security at Roswell Park and took an 80 percent pay cut, I felt pretty confident in my choice. Even with only rudimentary English, no formal education, starting at Roswell Park for only twenty-six dollars a week cleaning animal cages, I knew I would have opportunities to advance at Roswell.

However, I didn't take the position to do research; I didn't even know what research was. On the very first day, I joined the Health Research team of Roswell to support the doctors and technicians who did this experimental work.

And now, a small word of warning: much of what I have to say about my early days at the renowned Roswell Park Cancer Institute may sadden and shock you. Roswell is one of the oldest and most prestigious cancer research institutes in the United States, and when I started there in 1961, much of the research done there was considered cutting-edge. However, in those days, much of that experimental research was performed on live animals. Today this is very controversial, but back then it was the norm.

As I expected, this was not a pleasant job, but my dream drove me beyond my reservations. My past granted me a certain sense of confidence. A little boy who could keep his mother alive during a war could now become anything he set his mind to. I never allowed myself to take the easy or the lazy way out. I was a hard worker and I knew that about myself. I believed that a fresh start at Roswell might allow me to go as far as I wanted.

And it did. Happily, I can report that this was not a job with a short tenure like the others had been. I was able to fully express my entrepreneurial instincts at Roswell, albeit working within a large institution. My first instruction came from an elderly Ukrainian man who showed me how to clean the cages and provide food and water to the animals.

I started on a Monday morning. The weekend had provided the conditions needed for a breeding frenzy among the tiny inhabitants of the first cage I was to clean. I opened the cage door and within seconds, I was covered, head to toe, with baby mice. I screamed! They clung to my clothing so tightly, I had to strip and run away.

There was such laughter in the room! All the other caretakers were hysterical, nearly falling off their chairs, howling with laughter. "We've all been through it, too, Les. So, this is your baptism!" I was very cautious from then on.

The next incident was with the rats. The caretakers were explaining to me how to catch a rat. We did this with no gloves, by the way. So I reached in and sure enough, the rat bit me. As a matter of fact, he bit down and was hanging off my finger. My next lesson: When a rat bites you, its jaws lock and you cannot get it off you. Luckily, one of my co-workers came to my rescue.

Working at Roswell wasn't a picnic. During the first few days I wondered why I had traded the security of J.H. Williams for a day-to-day grind that involved cleaning up after monkeys, dogs, cats, rats and mice . . . had I left factory life merely to end up as a pooper scooper?

I continued to clean cages for a couple of months but I still hadn't met the boss, Dr. Ausman. I had met his gorgeous secretary, Kathy, however. She came to the lab one day. "Leslie, Dr. Ausman would like to see you."

I knew it. I was going to be fired.

Dr. Ausman narrowed his eyes and stared at me. "What are you going to do with your life?" he asked.

My factory experience had taught me that to be a real man in America you should talk tough, so I used every curse word I knew, thinking I would impress Dr. Ausman. He was a bit stunned and actually told me not to use those words.

I had blown it. I was sure it was the end for me at Roswell.

And then he said, "It looks like you are capable of doing far more than just cleaning the animal cages. How would you like to work with Bella and learn the trade?"

I nearly cried. "I thought you were going to fire me." He reassured me once more and that was that. I was on my way. Bella taught me how to do injections, anesthetize the animals, and, eventually, how to perform operations on the smaller animals. It turns out I had good hands for surgery, and I became a very good technician.

My salary nearly doubled. I was earning a whopping $48 a week now. However, money was not the goal . . . I was intent upon advancement.

I knew nothing about the anatomy of the animals I found myself working with, so I signed up for two night classes: Biology and Anatomy at Erie County Community College. I wanted to learn all I could about the work I was doing.

I was pretty proud of my accomplishments. Less than two years after I graduated from cleaning cages, I was operating on the inhabitants of those cages, developing surgical techniques that eventually would be used on human patients.

How do you explain this significant progress in such a short period of time? I've asked myself that question more than once.

Timing played a role. I happened to arrive at the very beginning of a new era in research, when there was a lot of opportunity for an aggressive, intuitive, and hard-working employee. But, it's also indicative of how I saw the world, and it's certainly proof that I was more than willing to step into this exciting environment, put myself at risk, and work to move forward.

Even when I began transplanting organs in animals, I was not earning as much as I had as a heavy equipment operator. But that was the least of my worries. I was advancing and I loved what I was doing. Life was good.

Once I learned how to operate on the smaller animals, I began to perform surgery on dogs and monkeys. I thought this was remarkable at the time, but I can only conclude that it was a logical outcome of a steady hand, hard work, practice, and most importantly, a commitment to my job.

I decided I wanted to become a surgeon. This was actually an old dream of mine, from when I was six years old in wartime Hungary. I really wanted to become a doctor, but you couldn't go to medical school at night, and I needed money to survive. I placed this dream on the back burner again and got back to work.

Nevertheless, I loved this job so much that I began to spend weekends in the library studying anatomy, pharmaceuticals, and other relevant topics. I became better and better at my job until I was promoted to a management role in the Health Research Experimental Surgery Department.

Because of my steady hands and experience, I specialized in kidney transplants, mostly on dogs. The secret to the survival of a foreign kidney is not so much the impact of the drugs used, but how quickly you take the kidney from the donor and get it connected to the recipient. Timing is crucial. Because of my speed and adeptness, I had a nearly one hundred percent success rate in these delicate procedures.

In fact, I wound up training medical students on how to do the surgery and kidney transplants on dogs and monkeys. I loved every minute of it!

Dr. Ausman observed my surgical skill time and time again, and on several occasions, brought an older gentleman with him to observe the techniques I used. One of the guest observers commented that he had never seen anything like this before. The guest turned out to be none other than Dr. Ausman's own father. The senior Dr. Ausman was a renowned surgeon who owned several hospitals in Chicago.

A flash went off in my mind, and a week later, I met with Dr. Ausman. I wondered if he would ask his father to be my sponsor to attend medical school. I actually pleaded with him. "I will not fail him, I promise. I need to go to medical school . . . I will pay him back and then some!"

When a Dream Dies

Dr. Ausman tried, but to my sorrow, he never did convince his father to sponsor me in medical school. That opportunity did not come about. I was forced to face it: my financial situation would not allow that particular dream to come true.

I worked with three or four research physicians: Dr. Nadler, Dr. Phalen, and several others. They explained to me what they needed in order to perform a certain experiment. For example, there are several veins in a mouse's tail. The challenge was to figure out how to inject a particular drug into just one of those veins. "Leslie, why don't you try to figure out how to do this procedure?"

So off I went to the library to start reading. I learned that if you put something in hot water, it dilates. Late one Saturday afternoon, I went to the lab. I anesthetized several mice, dipped their tails into warm water and sure enough, with my special glasses, I could see the veins dilate.

Once I found the veins, I had to figure out how to get a needle in just one. I worked until midnight and finally found that I could successfully perform injections into just the right vein.

On Monday morning, I called out, "Doc! I did it! I got the drug into the vein!"

He wrote a paper on the procedure and earned a lot of notoriety in the medical world. It turned out to be great! He mentioned my name, so I received even more recognition at Roswell, and became the expert on injecting drugs into mice tails.

I also received some recognition in the area of colon cancer. Often, when the physicians removed a tumor, the cells would spread and two or three years later, a tumor would reappear. "Leslie, figure out what we can do to prevent this. You will have to experiment again."

So once again I spent my weekend in the library.

I remembered what I had learned in school about liquid nitrogen. I felt it might just work to freeze the mass to keep all the cells intact during the operation. It was already known that freezing a tumor reduced the risk that individual cells might migrate during surgery, but it wasn't obvious how to accomplish this, especially in the colon. That was my assignment.

I went to the pharmacy and picked up a dozen or so condoms because they stretch and are flexible. I filled them with water to find out just how far they could stretch. I had to figure out how to implement this concept. I drilled two holes in a big cork and added tubing so that water could go in one side and out the other using an electric pump. The pump's purpose was to circulate the solution in the condom. I ran test after test on these condoms, to see how much solution could be added without breaking them. I actually had to double them so they could hold the required amount of solution and not burst. It took a lot of experimenting and dozens and dozens of condoms.

At the pharmacy, there was a pretty pharmacist. Eventually she could no longer resist. She asked, "What are you doing with all of these condoms?"

"Come on up to my lab on the seventh floor and I will show you," I replied. She, of course, never showed up!

After extensive testing, I did a trial using the more expensive liquid nitrogen. I didn't say a thing to Dr. Phalen until I knew precisely how much liquid nitrogen these could hold and how I would proceed with the actual experiment. Finally, I was ready. I drew a picture of a colon with a tumorous growth attached to the outside of the colon wall. I drew another illustration showing how the condom, complete with the cork assembly, would be slipped into the colon just below the tumor and circulate the liquid nitrogen until the tumor froze and the surgery was done. The physician would then be able to cut the tumor out without the fear of scattering any of the cancerous cells. Speed and precision were required.

This technique was perfected on animals and later used on human patients. I would have jumped at the opportunity to do these surgeries, but, since I was only a technician, I was not allowed. "Real doctors" were required.

I did, however, become part of the operating team when they decided to use this method on humans. My responsibility was to prepare the pump and manage it during the operation. I was very jealous that I was not one of the doctors performing the surgery. It was all so conflicting. I was very proud that I had helped develop this groundbreaking procedure to more safely address colon cancer, but I was frustrated that I could not do the actual procedure myself.

Forces Greater than Our Own

As fate would have it, Dr. Ausman decided to give up his research practice to accept the position of Director of Health Research in Roswell Park. One of his responsibilities was to automate the entire hospital.

I was sad to see our working relationship come to an end. During a visit with Dr. Ausman, at which I thought we were saying farewell, he suddenly became very serious. "Les, I would like to offer you an opportunity to change professions, and join the data processing department."

"But I have trained as a lab technician, Dr. Ausman. What do I know about computers? Why would you want me?"

"I'll tell you why," he said. "Because you are very talented. Any challenge that has been given to you, you've faced and completed. Think about it. What did you know about lab work or surgery before you joined us? All my doctor partners praise you day and night, but you are never going to make any money where you are without a Ph.D."

The words "never going to make any money" sounded horrible and harsh. The reality shook me, and I began to sense a change of heart. "I'd like to make much more money, it's true," I said. So, very reluctantly, but out of necessity, I accepted the transfer and moved over to the Data Processing Systems Department of Roswell. And that is how I got into the computer field. It was also the final blow to my dream of becoming a surgeon. Dreams do not die easily, however. It was a bittersweet pill to take.

I was still not making the $125 a week that the factory work had paid. But my wife, Kathy, was working, too, so we were able to share financial responsibilities.

I was learning, and that was something I always valued. I learned COBOL, FORTRAN, BAL, and RPG – the key programming languages of that era. And just as Dr. Ausman had predicted, I picked up the technology quickly. I also found I had a lot to offer the department based on my experience in hospital applications.

I wound up working for Dave Baer, the Director of Data Processing. We got along very well. He promoted me to Systems Analyst, and I was trained on computer operations. I learned a little of everything. At the time, Roswell was already a nationwide leader in the automation of medical records. So taking a bit of a risk to achieve a leadership role as Dr. Ausman began the campaign to automate the entire hospital turned out to be a very good move.

In 1963, RCA began to install a mainframe computer at Roswell, one of the first such installations in a facility like ours. Later we migrated to IBM computers. This was pivotal for IBM, as Roswell became the first installation of this magnitude in a hospital. Dr. Ausman was delighted to have the greatest computers and their providers as part of Roswell's overall medical records automation initiative.

In addition to being very creative, Dave Baer was also very good at hiring the proper person for each job, and he forged good working relationships with everyone in the department. Randy Marks, the sales rep for IBM, was working to unseat RCA as the computer vendor at Roswell. He and Dave Baer had an excellent relationship, and when everything was well underway, the two of them decided to leave Roswell to start their own business. Thus was born Computer Task Group, a computer consulting company that would come to be known as CTG.

ELEVEN | TRIUMPHANT RETURN TO HUNGARY

During this time, it wasn't all work and no play. I convinced my boss to let me take time off to visit my parents. I was finally able to get up enough courage to venture back to my country from which I had fled ten years earlier.

In 1966, I returned to Hungary as a proud U.S. citizen. I flew to Vienna, where I rented a small Volkswagen and prepared to cross the border at Hegyeshalom. When I saw the Iron Curtain and the stern-faced soldiers, I suddenly felt like there was no way I would ever return to Hungary. I fled to a small hotel nearby and spent the night pondering whether or not I should cross the border. The next day, trembling with fear, I braced myself and entered the country.

It was a harrowing experience. I was interrogated harshly; guards to the right, to the left, in front and behind me pounded me with sensitive questions. The Border Patrol wanted to catch me in just one misstep so they could turn me away. There was no way they wanted an escapee to return with tales of the freedom and opportunities that were available in other countries.

In Austria in 1966, debating whether to go over the border into Hungary for the first time since my escape.

My luggage and car were inspected meticulously. They even took the tires off the car to see if I had stashed something inside them. They could not find a thing. They had to let me go with one final warning . . . I was ordered to show up at the police station once I arrived in Győr. They wanted to track my every step, so they demanded that I report where I was at all times.

That was a small price to pay for being both home and free! I was driving through the countryside, happy as a lark, singing away when I noticed an old peasant woman with a scarf covering her head and a basket in her hand. She was bringing lunch to the fields for her husband. I offered her a ride, but she was visibly scared, unsure if this would be safe. She had never been in an automobile before, much less with a stranger. Always the salesman, I talked and talked until she felt safe enough to get in.

I will always remember her words as we set out to find her husband, "This goes automatically?" We both laughed! She was amazed.

I drove her to where her husband was slaving away. She was so grateful that she asked me to join them for lunch. They were having bacon, bread, sweet peppers and onions with a glass of wine. I thanked them for the wonderful meal, and then I got back on the road, anxious to see my parents and family.

As I drove, I thought about all the years since I had seen my parents, since the last time I saw their faces or gave them a hug. Even their voices were faint since we had only spoken a few times over the phone. They didn't have a phone in their home so I was only able to talk to them when they were at my sister Klári's house. For more than ten years I had been carefully writing and reading letters to keep them close to me. However, since the government censored all mail, it was difficult to write my true feelings.

The big welcome was incredible! Talking, crying, hugging . . . I was home! My mother was cooking and my father brought some of his best wine to the table. He had quite the stash, from all his friends. Although it was not the house that we grew up in, sitting at the dinner table with my parents and sister after all of those years truly felt like home.

Two days later, I faced another interrogation. My father warned me in advance: "Lacikám, this is going be a bumpy ride!" And he was right. A tall, broad, female officer, a real Amazon, in a leather-lined, soundproofed room fired the first question at me: "Why did you leave this country?"

A family portrait in 1966 during my first visit to Hungary after my escape. From left to right: me, my sister Ildi, my mother, my father, and my sister Klári.

Thank God I react quickly and think clearly in tough situations. "Ma'am," I said, intentionally avoiding the title "comrade" because it sickened me. "My parents gave me a hard time. We had many disagreements and it came to a breaking point. I felt like I could not take it anymore, so I chose to go west to escape my dysfunctional family."

It felt terrible to make such horribly untrue statements about my parents, but I had no choice. I certainly couldn't tell them that I hated the Communist regime. They asked me what I did in the U.S.; I told them my job involved working with computers.

When I was released, I recounted my lies to my father, sobbing through the whole confession. "Lacikám, you're a pretty clever boy!" he exclaimed, and I cried with relief. He understood and forgave me. Meanwhile, my mother was walking by and overheard the conversation. She immediately went into her bedroom and I could hear her saying a prayer asking for forgiveness for me. I loved her for that.

I visited all of my relatives including my other sister Klári, who no longer lived at home. My father asked me to go with him to his favorite place, a little Benedictine Catholic high school in the mountain town of Pannonhalma, where he had attended school.

It was there, beneath the trees, that we started to get to know each other, man-to-man, without government censorship. In the old days, we were made paranoid by the Communist regime. We were not allowed to speak about anything of consequence anywhere—not in public, not in private. No politics, no emotions, no family history, no personal thoughts could be expressed in our homes. You could be taken away and punished if you were overheard.

But on this special day, my father and I started to become friends. I could now explain to him why I chose to leave Hungary. When I fled, I was concerned that my father might run into trouble with the authorities and would be accused of having prior knowledge of my plans. Of course, he knew nothing of it. And, indeed, the Communist bullies did come after him and beat him mercilessly. Even though he eventually lied and confessed to having known my plans, he was tortured so badly that he ended up in the hospital.

This revelation brought me great sorrow. I could only say, "Dad, you should have lied right from the start! I am so sorry that I didn't know . . . I wish I had known, I wish I could have come back to help you."

I spent two weeks at home with these kinds of heartfelt conversations. You can imagine how I felt at the end of the visit. I was sorry to leave them again. I was sorry for their suffering. I was sorry for the

Friends and family saying good-bye in 1966, at the end of my first visit to Hungary.

loneliness they felt. Saying goodbye was gut-wrenching. Farewell was hard; it always is.

I promised myself that one day I would buy my parents a house in the lovely little village of Pannonhalma.

A Memorable Wedding

In 1968, one of my fellow escapees, Tivadar (Tibi), my friend from Kiskőrös, and I traveled to Hungary. We drove all the way from Frankfurt and stayed one night at my parent's home in Győr, where he met my younger sister, Ildi. Two years later, he went back to Hungary and married her. For the longest time, I wasn't even aware that Tibi was dating her. They had a huge wedding in Győr, which Kathy and I attended.

That's where I met the parents of my future brother-in-law. Tibi transported his parents from Kiskőrös in his small car. Tibi's mother brought along four or five live chickens as a gift. "My little chickens," was how she called to them. When Tibi's father lit a cigarette, and rolled down the window, the chickens hopped out at once, landing on the highway during rush hour. Tibi's father and mother were running around, dodging cars, wheels screeching, trying to collect the chicks. It was hilarious . . . two grown-ups running helter-skelter yelling, "chickie, chickie, chickie, here chickie," while traffic lurched to a halt. The next day, Tibi's mother made a feast from the chickens. They would never run away again.

The wedding was lovely. Six months later Tibi and Ildi set up life in Buffalo. They have been happily married ever since with two beautiful children, Judy (my goddaughter) and Tivadar (Ted), and four grandchildren. Our families and children are very close to this day and we have been able to spend the holidays and many other wonderful occasions together. Ildi reminds me of our home in Hungary and I am blessed to have one of my sisters so close.

– Laszlo Meszaros

TWELVE | KNOWING WHEN TO MOVE ON

was working on programming the hospital records when Dr. Ausman called me into his office once again.

"I have a special project, Leslie, and I need you to be in charge of it. I have just received a Federal grant to fund the development of a countywide Mercy Flight program for Buffalo. Mercy Flight is a fleet of helicopters that will be used to save people's lives when they have been in an accident and need to be transported for emergency medical care.

"There is one condition, however. I must make a commitment to work with the Buffalo Police Department. I need accident data and someone to set up statistics showing where and why these accidents are happening. I am going to assign this project to you. You will have to study and come up with a computerized system for accident reporting. You will do this via Roswell, as our employee."

Buffalo Police Department

I accepted the assignment and starting spending day after day at the Buffalo Police Department. It was a real challenge to automate every accident report on file for the previous fifty years. Dr. Ausman told me to hire a consultant to come in and help me implement the project as soon as I could. It was not easy. These paper reports were handwritten and, often, illegible. And the language in these reports? You don't even want to know!

To whom did I turn to for help? Computer Task Group (CTG). I went straight to Dave Baer and I hired consultants, clerks, and all kinds of people to work under my supervision, as Dr. Ausman had instructed. With the help of CTG, we did all the data processing for fifty years of accidents. Six or seven hospital employees, including my first wife Kathy, worked as programmers.

However, there was so much going on at Roswell that few employees were available to help with my project, so I relied heavily on CTG personnel.

Buffalo Police Department 911 Emergency Center. I am standing on far right next to Dr. Ausman, who took me under his wing at Roswell Park Cancer Institute.

By the time the project was completed, I had come to know the top echelon of the Buffalo Police Department. And a wonderful additional benefit was that Randy Marks, Dave Baer, and I had become good friends.

Dave's family and my friends and family have spent many memorable times together throughout the years. I love the way he describes spending time with the Hungarian group, since many of my American friends have had similar experiences.

As Dave describes our friendship: "From the beginning of our relationship, Les and I enjoyed a strong, natural friendship. As friends do, we both extended the friendship to include family and our close friends, as well. My fondest and most lasting of this spreading network of friends was our introduction into the Hungarian culture by Les and his friends.

Bean Soup (*Csülkös Bableves*)

"I think that my first exposure to Les and Kathy's hospitality and cookery was a dinner at the Meszaros' home featuring a wonderful bean soup, called *Bableves* Bublavash, and Chicken Paprikash. I went home in love with that dish.

"I'm not certain that the wine and dinner had anything to do with it, but the next day I took a fall while ice-skating, broke a femur, and spent the next six months in a leg and body cast."

I went to visit Dave Baer just before his surgery. I smiled at him as he was being wheeled in and he looked up, in his drug-induced stupor, pointed his finger my way and said repeatedly, "Bab leves, bab leves, bab leves!" He finally disappeared behind the surgical doors, but I will never forget these parting words . . . Bean Soup!

"The lesson learned?" says Dave. "Don't do anything hazardous after a big Hungarian meal!"

– Laszlo Meszaros

"We attended their parties, dinners, dances, and when the wine flowed, they drifted back to their native land recounting tales of family, church, school, wars, Russian occupation, escape, tradition, and song. They would sing of great events, both inspirational and saddening. There is nothing as mournful as a group of inebriated Hungarians, arm-in-arm, singing sad songs from the homeland. Hungarians are very emotional people, we learned, much more so than Americans."

As the Mercy Flight project wound down, Randy and Dave began trying to persuade me to leave Roswell and join them at Computer Task Group. When they offered me a much better salary, I really had no choice but to join CTG, a start-up with a staff of fewer than ten people. That was in 1969.

However, it was hard to leave the good people at Roswell and I felt guilty and sad. But I wanted this new challenge and Roswell simply could not provide me with that. When I met with Dr. Ausman to tell him the news, like a true gentleman, he shook my hand and warmly wished me well in my new endeavors. Dr. Ausman gave me tremendous opportunities to progress in my career. I will always be grateful to him.

Computer Task Group

Because of the success of the accident reports automation project, the Police Department began asking CTG what it would take to computerize all of their other records. At this point, Erie County Executive Ed Regan, got involved. "If you are going to do this for the City of Buffalo Police Department, then it should be county-wide," he said.

CTG received a Request to Bid on computerizing all the criminal and accident records for the twenty-nine police agencies and the Erie County Sheriff's Department. The really challenging part of the project was to design a system that allowed these agencies to share all of this information while ensuring the security of each agency's records. It was a very touchy situation. Computerizing sensitive police information was unheard of at that time. I had to build a trusting relationship with all the police chiefs before they would give their blessing to integrate police records with all the departments. Some information would also be shared with the New York State Criminal Justice computer system and the FBI's computerized database. Each agency needed to be assured that their private information would continue to be accessible only to that organization.

We wrote a grant to the Law Enforcement Assistance Administration in Washington for $1.5 million to study the feasibility of computerizing these records for all agencies to create a single computer system. CTG was awarded that contract, and I began assembling the staff to start working on a five-year plan for the county.

CTG was struggling at that time, so this project may have saved the company by providing a solid, multi-year foundation of project revenue.

Everyone at CTG celebrated. There were even champagne toasts! I headed up the project, and when we had completed the planning phase, I was asked to make a presentation to the County Executive and the Legislature on how to put services in place to fully support law enforcement. This proposal was passed by the Legislature, and the County took the proper steps to implement the plan.

Dave Baer and I described what a Data Processing Department should look like, the leadership positions and the technical staffing that would be needed, the background and experience that each employee should have, the salaries that should be offered, and the types of computers and facilities needed to support the operation.

We explained the potential of a computerized system and how it would benefit and support law enforcement in fighting crime. By providing them with up-to-date information on stolen vehicles, all arrests made to-date, criminals wanted countywide, real-time criminal histories, and delinquent parking tickets, law enforcement would be improved.

The County Legislature approved the proposal and made a commitment to continue the program after the grant money ran out.

During this time, my personal life began to flourish again and I met my beautiful wife Donna. We started a family, which quickly fueled my motivation for continued career success.

Central Police Services

In 1974, County Executive Regan formed Central Police Services (CPS). CPS was comprised of four branches: Communications, Centralized Training, Laboratories, and Information Services. During the search for a Director of the Information Services Division that housed the countywide computerized system, County Executive Regan suggested that the man who was responsible for securing the grant and legislative approval for the complex IT plan be hired. One of his lieutenants offered me the position.

I weighed the pros and cons. CTG was a viable company, but I was not an owner and I had no stock in the company. I was just another employee. So, I once again found myself taking a significant cut in pay—twenty-five percent, this time—to advance my career. I said yes to County Executive Regan.

I had convinced the County Legislature of the value of the project, but now I had to persuade the sheriffs and twenty-eight police departments that there were advantages to sharing their most critical information, such as criminal activities, incident reports, stolen vehicle and property reports, repossessions, and parking violations. The job gave me a lot of visibility, and required all the salesmanship I could muster.

It was also necessary to access information in real-time from the Department of Criminal Justice in Albany and from the FBI's computer systems in Washington D.C. These agencies all supported the initiative, welcoming the integration and understanding the advantages of such a collaborative approach.

I eventually built a staff of more than one hundred professionals, supplemented by consultants. From among the several qualified consulting firms, I chose my former company, CTG. It was the most qualified to do the job, and a critical level of trust already existed.

At CPS, we were on fire! We developed a prototype data sharing system for law enforcement agencies that police departments and computer vendors alike respected, and we gained national recognition all the way up to the FBI. This was all developed on a Univac system (which had purchased RCA), not IBM or NCR (National Cash Register). The prod-

At my desk at Central Police Services.

uct was proven, and the model was accepted by law-enforcement countywide, so all three of these top computer companies wanted to promote this system. They invited me to visit police departments throughout the country to do presentations on how computers can help fight crime and the benefits of using such a system. I promoted the Buffalo prototype and the concept. Those were the glory years in that position and I very much enjoyed that period of my career.

Eventually, the CPS IT system reached maturity. All applications were functioning, the management staff was trained and capable of taking over should I ever decide to leave. There were no new developments on the horizon due to budget limitations. The challenge was gone and all that was left was to manage the staff.

The exciting part of my County civil service job had evolved into a less desirable position. I was now handling only the problems that others faced when setting up their IT service programs and occasionally their personal problems, as well. I sat in my office, like a babysitter, no longer doing anything creative or entrepreneurial. There was no growth or innovation on the horizon and all the excitement of the job was gone. I was bored.

CTG, meanwhile, had become a thriving $25 million-a-year IT company. Thankfully, my friendship with Randy Marks and Dave Baer had continued during my tenure with CPS. We had even started a Gourmet Club together.

One evening, Dave, Randy, and I were having dinner at my house when Dave turned to me and said, "Les, how about we get back together and start a law enforcement department within CTG? We could take the system nationwide."

Just when I was feeling down, wondering what to do next, out of the blue came an offer that set my entrepreneurial spirit on fire again.

I decided to take Randy and Dave up on their offer. I replaced myself with Peter Matheisz, a very capable manager with the County. Peter was my brother-in-law from my first marriage and is one of my closest friends to this day. I returned to CTG in 1979 with a big title: Manager of Law Enforcement Systems, and an even bigger salary. Wearing my new CTG hat, I spent most of my time in Albany and Washington D.C., visiting police agencies to find opportunities and grants to increase business for my division.

Less than a year later, CTG installed a new president, Dave Campbell, and Randy Marks became chairman. Campbell decided to cut costs, keeping on only billable employees. He called me in one afternoon. "Les, I have to cut the budget, and I am sorry to say, we have decided to cut staff. We are terminating the Law Enforcement Division, and along with that we have to terminate your position, as well."

On September 24, 1980, I was let go. I was devastated. The two owners were very good friends, but I learned that day that there is no friendship in business. I had a wife and two children to support. I could have plummeted into depression, but instead an old dream rose to the surface. Reconnecting to this dream kicked my resilience back into gear.

Trust Your Intuition

For years, I had been sensing a desire, a mere whisper in my ear . . . start your own business, Les. This voice had been getting louder and louder. It is what kept me from going to the competition and offering my services. Instead, I risked everything to compete against CTG in a very professional way.

I knew I could be a success in business, doing a better job than most of the companies I had worked for. And, I told myself, if the worst happens and

I don't succeed, at least I know I took a shot at my lifelong dream. I could always get another job.

It was fairly audacious to try to compete against CTG. However, that was the industry I knew and most of my business contacts were in that field. So even though CTG was the dominating force in the information services industry in Buffalo, I decided to go up against them—head on! I am proud to report that I never poached a single CTG employee; there was no malice in my actions. Letting me go simply proved to be the kick I needed to take the final step towards self-sufficiency and success.

I saw my career path to this point as a series of zigzags; every time I had seen an opportunity, I had taken it. Several times I took a cut in salary to take advantage of an opportunity if I believed it was a necessary step to gain the momentum that would propel me forward.

To an outsider, these cuts in position and salary might have looked like failure, but they were actually part of my formula for success: take advantage of every opportunity to learn new concepts, make new connections, and advance in your industry, regardless of the fiduciary or administrative setbacks. They are only temporary. Just as the kicker in football hangs back before making his move, these setbacks are actually preparation for propelling yourself to future success.

THIRTEEN | **THE COM-PRO YEARS**

It is amazing how things just seem to happen in our lives. When you least expect it, something critical falls into place. I have learned to rely on this. Some call it luck; I call it faith.

My son Christopher played on a local hockey team. As do most fathers, I attended many practices and most of his games. During one fateful game, I met another faithful dad. We got to chatting and began to compare notes on our careers. "Why don't you come to my office," he said. "We can discuss my recruiting business. If you're interested, maybe you can join me, perhaps even become my partner."

I took him up on the offer and did some recruiting specifically for data processing personnel for a few months. We were doing well, but I soon discovered the economic reality of working alone: there are a limited number of hours in the day. A portion of each day is spent on marketing, selling, and performing overhead tasks, so not all of the hours are billable. This places a limit on the amount of money that one individual can make working as an independent consultant.

While it was necessary for me to roll up my sleeves, become billable, sell my services, and work for clients, it was never my final objective. My vision involved the acquisition of new clients and bringing on talent to serve those client needs, all with the hope of creating another CTG-like company and making sure to provide a good future for my family.

I believe that true entrepreneurs are entrepreneurs from birth, some just waiting to awaken. At some point in your life, you discover that your innate talent and desire is to become your own boss. However, that may not necessarily happen at the optimal time to drop everything and start a business. It is essential to look for the right opportunity, and the right time.

I knew I was an entrepreneur; I knew I could start my own business. By adopting a different set of values and a different set of operating principals, I knew I could compete effectively. The opportunity did not present itself until CTG fired me in 1980 and the new recruiting/consulting opportunity arose. I realized that it was the right time for me to go it alone.

The Birth of Com-Pro

My wife Donna and I had numerous discussions about my desire to start my own business. I couldn't sleep and continued to wrestle with this dream. We decided together that this was the time to start the business. Since we only had five thousand dollars in savings in the bank, we agreed there would be no additional expenses or luxuries for the next six months and that we would reevaluate our situation at that time.

My home office.

I came up with the name Com-Pro, an abbreviation for Computer Professionals. My first consulting assignment was with Marine Midland Bank doing systems analysis. It went well. In just a short time, I developed a good relationship with the client. They liked my work, but there were not enough hours in the day to do it all. My main focus became, not generating billable hours for myself, but rather on finding opportunities in the bank for more openings for additional consultants.

I convinced the Bank's management that they would be better off if I brought in additional talent capable of doing the same caliber of work as I was providing, if not better. I offered to supervise them and become their non-billable, independent project manager. They agreed to the deal, and I started recruiting, filling positions and slowly building a staff of computer professionals.

And then I had what I look back on now as a stroke of genius, based perhaps on my brief experience in the world of recruiting. I changed the way Com-Pro contracted with its clients. In that era, most "body shops" took great care to hold on to their people. Contracts with clients generally included prohibitions against "poaching," and it wasn't uncommon for consulting companies, including CTG, to sue clients to retain staff.

I implemented the exact opposite strategy. I expressly permitted clients the option of hiring our consultants away from Com-Pro after one year of continuous contract work, assuming appropriate notice was given. This fresh approach fully differentiated Com-Pro from its competitors, including CTG. It did not take long for Com-Pro to assemble a fiercely loyal core group of clients. Ironically, Com-Pro's turnover rate was actually lower than that of its competitors, which worked so hard to prevent "poaching."

Again, something bigger than myself was working away in the background of my life. One evening I bumped into Peter Tomasello at a local pub. Peter had been the RCA onsite IT Communication Specialist and account representative for the CPS account at the same time that I was the Director of Information Services for CPS.

It was fate to now meet again. I had left CTG a few months earlier, and Com-Pro was in start-up mode. Peter had recently left RCA and was working as an independent consultant. By that time, I was already providing professional services to a few clients with a handful of employees. I knew this wasn't a "one-man job," and that I needed to expand, so this meeting was very timely. I needed a partner, and Peter seemed like a good candidate for the position.

With my Com-Pro partner, Peter Tomasello.

As Peter recalls it, "Les, you were very determined about what was required for the IT enterprise. You could be a bit tough to deal with at times, but in the end, you were very fair and one of RCA's best accounts." He said all of this with a smile on his face.

I had both strategic and tactical business experience, as well as influential business contacts. Peter had tactical business experience and a strong IT technical background. As the conversation continued well into the evening in my wine cellar, my collection of homemade wines was rapidly diminishing. Peter and I shook hands, and the next day we were partners. The following day we sat down and put together a strategic plan on how to grow Com-Pro.

Our motto? "Whatever it takes!" Peter and I worked together to handle sales, recruiting, contracts, and employee and sub-contractor agreements. In addition, I handled financing, accounting, and running the company.

We hit it off immediately and worked well as a team. I had a vision for the company that translated into a focused strategy. Peter had tactical and technical skills that were a perfect complement.

The two of us very quickly discovered ways to minimize overhead. Initially, the company grew in Buffalo using local talent with local clients, but there was a natural cap on what the Buffalo market could sustain. Expansion into new cities was the next logical step. Peter and I were both more than willing to get on a plane, go to a different city—Tampa was our first target—and work out of a hotel room making sales calls. We would work on site until just enough local business was acquired to rationalize opening a local office, ultimately transitioning it to a local branch manager.

Peter, a brilliant technical lead, and I, the consummate salesman, worked well together. Within four years, Com-Pro was operating very successfully in Buffalo, Rochester, Tampa, and Orlando. We had more than 300 systems engineers whose time and effort were being billed out to major companies, including M&T Bank, Delta, Kodak, Xerox, Disney, and many more. Com-Pro had grown from a one-man operation to a four-city operation with a large inventory of contracts, a talented staff, and a great reputation. The company was generating fifteen percent pre-tax profit, which was unheard of for this type of business. We had structured the business to be able to capture new opportunities very quickly.

The business formula was working. I kept putting myself into new situations, giving myself new challenges and risks. I carried forward what I learned, along with the people I had met along the way, gleaning everything I could from each experience. I listened to both clients and employees, trying to understand all of their comments and respect their input. Smart CEOs listen.

This was Peter's M.O., as well as mine. We would wring all the benefits and wisdom out of these experiences, and then move forward to the next rich field of possibility, hoping to leave each place better than when we arrived.

One thing that differentiated Com-Pro from similar companies was the absence of central control. In fact, an organizational chart of the firm made it look a bit more like a network or a "crowd" than a corporation. Neither top-heavy nor bottom-heavy, this type of "flat" organization allowed us to create new branches in new cities at a very low cost. It also permitted us to close a branch very economically should it under-perform.

All of this was accomplished without external financing. Starting from scratch, Peter and I patiently assembled a very competitive and profitable company the old-fashioned way – by acquiring opportunities and managing those opportunities so they would fund themselves.By this time, I was no longer billing any of my time working as a systems analyst. My sole focus was leadership, management, and growth. I was the first line of the business, operating front and center to draw in clients, talent, and commitment to the projects.

Business in Hungary

While building Com-Pro in the U.S., I decided to also venture into the business landscape of my homeland. Com-Pro was still in its early stages, but I managed to pool enough money to buy my parents a house in Pannonhalma, the village where my father and I had our first heart-to-heart talk following my escape to America. Every time I visited them, Pannonhalma was the first place we went. I not only bought a house across from a monastery for my father, but I made sure it was spacious enough for my sister Klári and her husband Erno to live with them. It was win-win, ensuring that my elderly parents would have the help they might need.

During a visit, I was introduced to Áfész in Körmend, a publicly held agricultural corporation. I was convinced to form a joint venture and build a hotel at the back of my father's garden, facing the monastery. I imposed two conditions: first, should my parents die, the house would be passed on to Klári and Erno. Second, Klári and Erno would be employed at the hotel, to ensure that they would be provided for financially. The hotel could have been an excellent workplace for them for the rest of their lives.

The Pax Hotel, as we named it, had thirty-six rooms, and I was a minority proprietor. At that time, Hungarian law specified that a U.S. citizen could only become a minority investor, the only reason I agreed to such a transaction. In hindsight, this was a really bad business decision. I should never have agreed to a minority position. This left me helpless when problems arose. I had the best of intentions, but I was at a disadvantage.

Once the construction was done, the Hotel Pax opened. We sealed a contract with the Monastery by shaking hands, as they seemed offended at the prospect of a written contract. It stipulated that the Monastery would occupy sixty percent of the rooms, which they really needed.

Unfortunately, I was unable to take part in the Opening Ceremony. Based on a recommendation of the corporate manager, a young hotel manager who spoke English and German fluently was hired. I spoke with him by phone, and he seemed like a capable candidate.

HUNGARY   PAX HOTEL   PANNONHALMA

The Pax Hotel in Pannonohalma, Hungary in 1990.

The manager organized the Opening Ceremony, to which he invited half a dozen Benedictine priests from the Monastery. However, the manager made a terrible mistake. He put holy images, religious books and magazines in one set of bookshelves, catering to the priests who would reside there. But he put Playboy magazines in another bookcase, presumably catering to the hotel guests.

But it gets worse! The priests wanted to inspect the rooms, but what they found were condoms and tampons next to the soap. That put an end to the business relationship with the Monastery and thus an end to the profitability of the hotel. I received a letter from the priests telling me how disappointed they were. Had I been there, I could have prevented this. The head of Áfész who was there at the ceremony, could also have prevented all this from happening, but she did nothing. The hotel was effectively ruined.

It opened for business, nonetheless, but business never materialized. The hotel manager proceeded to engage in some very shady practices. For instance, he made a deal with taxi drivers in Győr to transport people who were engaged in illegal activities to the hotel. He demanded cash, which should have been a clue.

My sister and brother-in-law alerted me to the fact that many guests weren't registered in the hotel's accounting. They knew something shady was happening. I may have been a minority owner, but I was invested in the success of this hotel.

I decided to go to Hungary to investigate personally. Within a matter of weeks, my wife and I were on a trans-Atlantic flight. Since the hotel manager had not yet met us, we decided to check in as strangers and become detectives. I just needed to see him in action.

When we arrived, we went to the hotel bar and looked at the beverage menu. We said we would stay the night, but would like to have a cognac first. We saw no cognac at the bar, but the manager said, "No problem. I'll get some from the back office."

I asked Donna to go to the window to see what he was up to. I knew there was no back office. He opened the trunk of his car and pulled out a bottle, just as I expected. Donna then asked for some Bailey's. The shyster returned to his car again to get another bottle. When he was about to pour, I stopped him. "Not so fast. You don't have to pour anything for us. I am László Mészáros, and this is my wife. You're fired, effective immediately." The guy blushed and started trembling.

I gave him half an hour to pack up and leave. That was that. He was gone and we had to decide what to do next. Hire someone new and risk going through this again? Or lease the hotel and let someone closer take the responsibility?

We decided on the latter, but the renters turned out to be crooks, too. They stayed two or three months without paying one dollar of rent and then disappeared. I even hired an investigator to track them down, but they had transferred all their assets to their wives. So we lost additional income.

We tried one last time. Same scenario—the crooks won. I had no alternative but to put the hotel up for sale. I like to think that God stepped in again. A couple wanted to buy the hotel and the house as an investment for their daughter who wanted to return to her native Hungary from Germany to start a health spa. Pannonhalma was a quiet village in a beautiful area, very conducive to wellness.

So, that's the story of the hotel. My conclusion? Even successful business people make mistakes. My mistake was thinking not with my brains, but with my heart.

By the way, once both the house and hotel were sold, I made sure to provide Klári and Erno with a suitable place to live in Győr. Unfortunately, there would be many more mistakes to learn from in the business world ahead.

Diplomacy and a Team of Remarkable People

Early on, I realized that entrepreneurs must be great sales people. Since my childhood, when I bartered my sister's smiles for packs of cigarettes, I knew that I had a knack for sales. I was energized by the very thought of selling. After all, selling is a social activity, and I was, and still am, a very social person. I love the give and take, and I was very well-trained by my dad, who distributed farmland during a very tense and fragile time in Hungary. Those were volatile times, and yet he always remained on good terms with all parties.

My father taught me that it pays to use diplomacy. I learned at an early age how to manage a large number of sales prospects through to closure. But, even beyond all this, I intuitively understood that, when you build a company from scratch, leading it into several other cities, the line between your company and your personal identity is fairly thin. You are the company, and to a certain extent, the company is you.

The product that I sell most effectively is me. I look at the development of every business endeavor as an opportunity to create a new personal relationship—a trust relationship—between Les Meszaros and the client. A handshake means more to me then a contract. I know that once that bond is in place, I can direct my team to start building a positive and profitable relationship with the client.

As Com-Pro grew, it was necessary to put leadership and advisory capability in place. Peter and I assembled a team of key employees and outside consultants—legal, accounting, tax—so that we always had expert advisors to turn to. Those early advisors stayed with us through the duration of this business and beyond, forming the core of a true team.

I discovered this formula and perfected it at Com-Pro. In order to succeed in business—or in life—you have to surround yourself with knowledgeable people. You have to lead and challenge them, treat them as you would like to be treated. Finding great people is a huge undertaking, however, and the consequences of a bad hire can be disastrous. Both Peter and I felt that we had been given the gift of discernment, that we could assess a person quickly and accurately, making us very good at hiring. Or so we thought...

There were a few "bad apples" over the years at Com-Pro, but by and large, the story of Com-Pro is made up of remarkable people. We assembled a closely-knit, highly talented group, kept them challenged, and were therefore very successful.

I cannot over-emphasize the importance of people. My message is simple: hire people who are smarter than you are, provide leadership, delegate, challenge them, communicate, focus on integrity, and keep the emphasis on the customer.

A Few Scary Apples

Strictly by the numbers, we did a stunning job at Com-Pro acquiring and retaining talent. But—and I am the first to admit this—when you have an organization with more than 300 employees, it's almost inevitable that a few mistakes will be made.

Since a mistake is merely an opportunity to learn something, I am more than willing to share these stories, including one that's more than a bit scary.

Com-Pro achieved critical mass around 1986, so Peter and I decided to invest in someone to focus on strategic planning. For reasons that will become obvious, I'm going to redact the name of the individual. We'll call him John Doe. Treated as a case study, this is very likely the most disastrous hiring decision Com-Pro ever made.

Not only had Peter and I interviewed this man, but we had our key staff members meet with him, as well. He was charismatic, and dazzled everyone. He had significant technical capabilities, a photographic memory, and formidable financial skills. From the very start, everyone was impressed with his capabilities. However, in hindsight, there were a few red flags early on.

He was in the Special Services, a Ranger in the Army, and he was very intelligent. He was in seclusion for six months just to be debriefed before returning to civilian life. He was a computer expert with a photographic memory.

This man could perform wonders! He could look at a contract and in just minutes find the errors and discrepancies. He was brilliant. He was also lonely at times, so Peter or I would take him out for dinner with a few glasses of wine now and then, or for the occasional lunch, to get him away from the building and spend time with him socially.

The first hint that we might be in trouble came during one such lunch. As the meal progressed, John Doe started opening up more and more to me about his background as an Army Ranger. This in and of itself wasn't disturbing. In fact, we proactively searched for military retirees. They, along with competitive sportsmen, were most likely to have acquired the discipline and leadership skills needed in a small, fast-growing organization. I asked him about his Army stories, but I was a bit disturbed when he spent a good portion of lunch telling me about all of the training he'd had in hand-to-hand combat, including techniques to kill people with his bare hands.

He told me some frightening facts about being able to snap a person's neck and kill them in seconds. He said he was very good at it. He was proud of this ability. Every once in awhile, he stopped mid-sentence, as though he was remembering not to speak about a topic. He looked around and acted as though he was being watched. He said, "Some of us were able to fake it. Some of us retained everything we had been trained to do. If I don't like someone, like that guy, I could just walk up to him and finish him off."

Oh, shit, I thought. What is this all about? But, by then, he had caught himself and stopped talking. Although initially frightened, I let it go because his work was so valuable. He did a lot of good things for the company.

That summer, my wife and I took the kids on vacation to Muskoka Lake in Canada. When we returned, the office manager's car was in my driveway. She emerged from her car crying and shivering. "Les, we've got to talk!"

"What happened?"

"It's about John Doe. Last Friday, we were working late. At about 6 o'clock there was a knock on the door. 'This is the FBI, we are looking for John Doe.' I said he was in the back office. Six men jumped out of four unmarked cars, ran right past me into the back, handcuffed him, and took him away."

The office manager was shaking. She told me that he had pleaded with her, shouting, "Don't believe anything they say! I'm innocent." I didn't sleep all night. Donna was upset, too, but we never did tell the kids. The next morning I called the police. I needed to know what had happened. I was informed that this former employee of mine was wanted in another state for opening a clinic and pretending to be a doctor. That was crazy enough, but then I was told he was also being investigated for possibly killing his former business partner, execution-style, and leaving him in the trunk of a car. That was bone-chilling.

As had happened previously, the police were forced to let him go until they could collect enough evidence to arrest him. I was told I had to let him back into the office to work. In the meantime, I was cooperating with the police as they continued to investigate the crime, trying to obtain information that might help put him away. I did all this behind the back of a man who could kill me with his bare hands.

I knew that I had to let John Doe go, but I was legitimately scared. I suffered many sleepless nights and sat through many consultations with the police. The FBI tried to help. A strategy was set up with Buffalo law enforcement agencies to orchestrate the firing process. We came up with the excuse that we were losing money. His job wasn't crucial for the company's survival, so we had to let him go.

We picked a restaurant on Main Street to meet for breakfast. Undercover agents and plain-clothed police officers were strategically located in the restaurant. I was nervous but determined. I knew it had to be done. I acted as calm as I could knowing that I was about to fire a suspected murderer.

I recalled a lesson I learned at a very young age during the war: God gives strength to act under stress. It helped me collect my thoughts and jump into action. I was able to muster up the courage to calmly say, "I have some bad news for you. I was working on the budget and I realized that we're losing money. We're in trouble and I have to let some people go to decrease overhead." I had acted in plays as a youth, but for the first time I recognized my talent as an actor.

He said, "Does that mean me?"

I took a deep breath. "Yes, unfortunately, you and several others. We will go back to the premises and you can collect your things."

He said, "So fast?"

"Yes, it's the best way."

It was over. He packed up and went quietly. I was shocked that he didn't fight to stay. The entire experience bothered me for a long time. He was later arrested and found guilty.

Another trouble spot was Charlotte, North Carolina. A young man we had hired from IBM to work with us at Com-Pro wanted to move down south. He was smart, good looking, and clean-cut. He had made a commitment as branch manager to run the Charlotte office with integrity and honesty and to grow the business. He ran the branch, but we found out that he was also building his own consulting company while on Com-Pro's payroll. He had told everyone that the branch was a subsidiary of Com-Pro and that he was actually employing them and paying them based on their billable hours.

One of my clients asked me about this subsidiary. I was livid. I flew immediately to Charlotte to investigate. It was true . . . all of it was true. I confronted the manager and fired him on the spot. Com-Pro never did recover that business, but he had been working on such a thin profit that it wasn't a huge loss for the company. Unfortunately, we wound up closing that branch.

Growing the Business

The next challenge? How to grow the business. I decided that, instead of three to six months with extensions, we needed to sign longer commitments for our consultants from each client. With qualified Branch Managers at each site, we started focusing on expansion. We spent most of our time interviewing and searching for extraordinary recruits. It was challenging at times. An engineer could ace the interview, come to work for us, and then fall apart in the day-to-day.

Overall, though, we had just a three to four percent turnover rate per year. Other companies like ours had a turnover rate of as much as twenty-five percent. I attribute this to having set up the business as a family and treating everyone fairly. Management knew the employees, their children, and their family lives. It made a huge difference.

The industry at that time was switching from owning their own large computers to leasing them. I thought, how can I get involved in this end of the business, the leasing business?

Advisors and strategic partners were needed. After surveying the market, Peter and I noticed that many of our largest clients were signing long-term leases to fund the acquisition of their mainframe and mid-range computing equipment.

This put the onus on the client to separately acquire the hardware and the software from two different vendors. Peter and I were fully aware that Com-Pro was frequently providing the final piece of the puzzle—the solution that turned the hardware into a way to automate an activity within the corporation. We also understood that clients preferred to hold one person responsible for the delivery and servicing of that solution. To lengthen the engagements of our consultants, thereby creating longer and more strategic relationships with our clients, we came to the conclusion that forging a partnership with one of these leasing companies should be our next step.

Continent Information Services, CIS, in Syracuse, was the second largest computer leasing company. They leased systems for a full seven years. CIS stock was growing like crazy—they had a gold mine on their hands! The company was grossing $1.2 billion annually. We needed to get involved.

A meeting was arranged. Peter and I drove to Syracuse and put on a polished presentation illustrating how Com-Pro could act as a professional services arm for CIS. We suggested that Com-Pro begin by expanding throughout the CIS offices, financed by CIS. The two firms could collaborate, offering integrated services (hardware and software) to existing clients, therefore differentiating themselves from competitors. Com-Pro could lead its existing clients to CIS as new hardware was required. CIS could focus its solution selling with its new partner, gaining further control over their customers, as well as access to new sources of revenue.

The value proposition of this alliance seemed obvious to me, so I pitched it and asked for the order. What I didn't know was that a team of planners and analysts led by CIS CFO Robert Woodrow (who later became a good friend and valued mentor) had studied the market and come to the exact same conclusion. In other words, I walked into CIS and pitched them their own business plan. Whether this was plain dumb luck, brilliant planning, or a combination of the two, is irrelevant. Com-Pro was in the right place at the right time with exactly the right story.

Even as we walked out of the building, I knew we'd had a great meeting. The dynamics in the room made this evident, but more telling was that Woodrow had suggested that we meet him for lunch that same day. I assumed that this would be when we would close the deal and begin planning the expansion of Com-Pro in a strategic partnership with CIS.

That's not what Woodrow had in mind.

He was clear. "The only way I am going to go with this plan is if it's done internally. We will not enter into a partnership. I have been planning this for months. I put that plan together for us, where software and hardware are sold together, and I have been talking to and looking for consulting companies that would fit the mold, who would fit into the CIS culture."

We thanked him for his time and left. I was disappointed, since my idea was partnership, not acquisition. But Peter seemed thrilled. Back at the office, a call from CIS came in the next day. "Great meeting. Mr. Woodrow really liked you guys and would like to discuss a business relationship."

That was that. I talked to Peter and the rest of the management team, especially our CFO, Bud Crumlish, whose opinion and suggestions I valued and respected. As I shared the bad news and the good, I was shocked by Peter's response. "Hey, brother, let's sell!"

"No way," I said. "I am not ready to retire, and I am not at all ready to start up a new business. This is our baby, and we are just building it up."

"Yes, but think about it," replied Peter. "We never took much money for ourselves for all our hard work. Now we have the chance to get our money's worth!"

Peter and I continued to talk, and at the end of the day, I agreed to go back to Woodrow to hear the specifics of the offer.

Here's what he said: "Les, we will buy Com-Pro as a subsidiary. You will remain the President, and Peter will remain the Vice President. You keep all your management staff and we will give you a ten-year contract. I know that every branch costs money to launch, so we will cover the start-up costs to open additional branches. You will set up and run a companion professional services organization in every city where there is now a CIS office. You will never have to worry about capital for expansion."

There were CIS companies in about forty cities across the U.S. and Canada, and I had no doubt that we could fulfill our part of the plan with funding from CIS. The sale started looking pretty damned good, even to me, especially when a pro forma offer to acquire Com-Pro was handed to me.

I decided to go back and meet with Woodrow, letting him know I might be open to selling. There was one key question, and I decided to ask it immediately. "What about the price?"

Cash is Always a Sure Thing

"Well, we can probably give you stock for your company, but I want to get management approval, and I need to do due diligence," was Woodrow's response.

I had never sold a business, so I did not know how to properly value one or how best to be paid. I reached out to Mark Sullivan who had handled Mergers and Acquisitions for Ernst and Young.

Woodrow turned out to be a formidable negotiator, but we finally came up with a dollar amount that he said was the best possible offer. Mark was also a tough negotiator, however, and he did not like selling for stock only. At one point, Mark came to me with this advice: "Cash is the sure thing."

The final decision regarding cash versus stock was up to me and I decided to heed Mark's sage advice. Eight years after starting the business in 1980, we sold it for cash. In 1988, Com-Pro was fully liquidated into CIS. We retained the right to run the subsidiary under the Com-Pro brand, and CIS had committed funding to expand Com-Pro under our leadership. Mark Sullivan was yet another landmark blessing in my life.

Another blessing gained during this experience was meeting Mr. Robert Woodrow. He was a remarkable man, so full of life and a veritable genius. Over the course of the next twenty-three years, Bob Woodrow and I would become close friends. His final message to me was heartwarming:

"Les, you have been a great influence on my life; and I have always considered you my role model. You are some guy, Les. I have many, many great memories of times we shared together."

Bob passed away in 2014, and I miss him dearly.

Work began smoothly. The biggest challenge was to hire the most competent talent who were also the kind of people who would fit into our family-style culture.

CIS had offered me a sizable yearly salary with all kinds of bonuses. In all honesty, the money I received from the sale was enough to take care of my family for a very long time. Peter and I were now both well-to-do, financially secure, even after taxes. I got to keep managing the business and continued the expansion, but it wasn't about money for me.

Instead of feeling elated, I realized I felt empty, as though I had just given away my baby. I also felt like I had betrayed my employees. I had gotten them bonuses, but we were no longer a close-knit family. I had sold off something I had worked very hard to build. I went through a period of soul searching, trying to figure this out.

A Man of Character

During my thirty-six years in public accounting, I was fortunate to meet and work with many wonderful people for whom I have a great deal of respect. Les is certainly one of them. He is also one of the few business relationships that grew into a lifelong friendship. Some highlights: visiting Budapest with Les and Donna and watching him sing with troubadours in the restaurants, taking a boat trip with them to Baltimore Inner Harbor with our personal U.S. Coast Guard escort,

Singing with a gypsy band in Hungary while traveling with Mark and Toni Sullivan in the late 1980s.

and being a guest at Erika's fabulous wedding and meeting Les's lifelong friends from all walks of life.

It was, however, the sale of Com-Pro that had the biggest and most lasting impression on me. In 1985-1986 I was between Price Waterhouse and Ernst & Young. I was operating under the cleverly creative business name "Mark L. Sullivan and Associates" and was primarily advising on Mergers and Acquisitions.

I had recently met Les and was assisting him on the potential sale of Com-Pro. I wasn't overly concerned with legal contracts and took assignments sealed only by a handshake. If somebody wanted to renege on a fee, it was on them, and their name and integrity apparently weren't worth very much. In certain cases, people would "rationalize" that the fee for a transaction was somehow less than what was agreed upon up-front. The M&A business was a feast or famine scenario. I was on the famine side of things at the time and was hoping that Les would be a stand-up guy in this Com-Pro transaction.

The day we closed on the sale of Com-Pro, on the ride back from Syracuse, Les pulled a pre-written check from his shirt pocket and said, "I believe I owe you this." It was to-the-penny what I had calculated.

That was the first of many times that Les proved to be a man of character and of the highest integrity. As a footnote on the sale, we went "old school" and insisted on an all cash deal from CIS. This proved to be fortuitous, as CIS went Chapter Eleven within eighteen months. I guess good things do happen to good people!

The more perspective we gain in life the more we appreciate how lucky we are to meet and befriend some truly wonderful people. To my good friend Les, *Egészségedre* (Cheers)!

– Mark Sullivan

I finally realized that, good deal or not, I had lost my authority. I was no longer calling the shots. In hindsight, it was another wake-up call. I just couldn't be happy as one small cog in a larger wheel.

Despite this epiphany and many misgivings, there was still a job to do. We needed to expand the Com-Pro subsidiary into every CIS office. But I also wanted to incorporate new types of business. I devised a strategy that required Com-Pro to hire a very small group of Business Development Specialists, each one having responsibilities in all of the branches, helping them generate new and different types of business.

My first priority was to find someone to help with the exploding telecommunications market. This was a high priority because CIS leased a lot of telecommunications equipment and Com-Pro needed to find ways to add value. I chose Bob Fritzinger to lead this effort.

Bob's background was a bit different from that of the typical consultant, but that was okay because I didn't intend to use him in the typical manner. He started his career in the classroom, and I felt reassured knowing that he could stand in front of a group of people and teach them the things I wanted them to know. And with his former employer, he'd been successful at working with clients to get new products launched.

The fact that he could teach, combined with his ability to innovate, meant he might be able to roam across all of the Com-Pro branches and help them develop entirely new lines of business to add to our revenues.

Bob suggested he teach the branches to begin working with voice mail and call centers, both of which were new systems and growing very quickly. The very first client was the result of a successful response to a Request for Proposal (RFP) from DuPont. We closed the deal and got to work.

Taking on the World of Telecommunications

In 1988, very few corporations used voice mail and fewer still owned their own voice mail systems. DuPont, however, used voice mail on a massive scale and was very innovative.

Voice mail includes two essential features and one very valuable option. At least two of these must work reliably or voice mail is useless. First and foremost, a voice mail system must handle all calls perfectly. It cannot answer a call with "Who would you like to leave a message for?" It must answer with something much more specific, like "Hi, this is Les Meszaros. Please leave your message after the tone." It's also very desirable for the voice mail system to identify the caller. That would allow Les, when he's listening to his message, to hear, "Message from Joe Smith at 7:30 a.m." instead of "Message at 7:30 a.m."

The other feature isn't quite as obvious, but it's often more important. When a message is left in a voice mailbox, the message lamp on the telephone must light up indicating that a message has been left. Otherwise, there's no reason to check for voice mail.

If both the phone system and the voice mail system are purchased from the same company, everything generally works well. But many corporations prefer to choose their own separate vendors. In 1988, if you bought voice mail from a company other than the one that manufactured the telephone system, calls were frequently not handled properly and message indicators failed to light up.

DuPont challenged Com-Pro to solve this problem.

At first glance, this seemed like an easy problem to solve, but it turned out to be much more complicated than we originally thought. It quickly became obvious that hardware would need to be designed and built to deliver a full solution.

Fortunately, David Straitiff, a brilliant young engineer, was already working at the Buffalo branch of Com-Pro on another contract. I shifted David over to help Bob with this project. Within just a few months they delivered a solution, ready to go to market. They named it VoiceBridge.

Com-Pro never had the opportunity to fully take this unique product to market, however. Eleven months into the marriage of CIS and Com-Pro, CIS declared Chapter Eleven bankruptcy.

My fiduciary responsibility was to work with the Bankruptcy Trustee to find a buyer for the Com-Pro division, but Bob and Dave kept pestering me, telling me that the product they had just designed could be turned into a rather significant business.

I faced a massive business dilemma.

Fiftieth Birthday Celebration

It was April, 1989, and I was turning fifty. I could not believe that I was a half a century old already, but I was too busy working to give it much thought. Fortunately, my incredible staff at Com-Pro were laying other plans.

It was a typical workweek, except that all of my branch managers from Rochester, Tampa, Orlando and Atlanta were in town for a corporate meeting. They had insisted on holding the conference on a Friday. On Saturday, we were going to close the activities with a night out enjoying champagne and a wonderful dinner to celebrate the progress of the company. The managers had even arranged to pick my family and me up at home in a limousine, so we could all enjoy our cocktails and not worry about getting home.

As soon as I got into the limo, one of the managers remembered that he had left something he needed at the office, so off we went. It was strange, though, because the limo driver stopped at the end of the parking lot . . . a bit away from the building and let the manager walk from there to the office building. I found it odd, but continued chatting with my family.

Only minutes after he entered the building, the doors opened wide and out flooded nearly two hundred people, singing, yelling "Happy Birthday!!" and waving their arms. "Surprise!"

At first, I didn't quite know what to make of it all, but it slowly dawned on me that this was a celebration for my fiftieth birthday! In the chaos of the moment, suddenly I heard music . . . it was perfect! The team had hired a three-piece band and they were out there on the driveway playing one of my favorite songs, "Don't Worry, Be Happy."

My surprise 50th birthday party at Com-Pro, given to me by my staff. More than 160 came to celebrate.

All my treasured employees were there, along with special friends, including a celebrity in the construction industry, Frank Ciminelli, and of course my family. Eventually, after I shook hands with everyone, we all went inside. I was astounded. The organizers of the event: Terry Wagner, recruiting director, and Connie Kaun, accounting manager, had arranged for the huge atrium to be decked out in colorful birthday decorations. There was even a head table, specially decorated for the guest of honor.

Several speeches followed by my key staff, Donna, and then Chris and Erika. My children had never given speeches before a crowd of this size before, and I found myself tearing up. I was so emotional and touched by it all. I immediately stood and delivered my heartfelt gratitude for this amazing party, and then, after a wonderful, catered dinner . . . we danced!

I was so impressed that my staff would honor me with such a huge shindig. A lot of work went into this festive occasion, and to this day, I still don't know how they managed to keep it a secret.

FOURTEEN | **FIRST STEPS TO SILICON VALLEY**

In the fall of 1989, I had to make a difficult decision. Should I figure out a way to buy back Com-Pro? Or should I leave my baby behind and start fresh with a new effort? My loyal staff wanted me to repurchase the company. But almost daily, either Bob Fritzinger or David (Dave) Straitiff nagged me about the importance of focusing on VoiceBridge, the new product developed for DuPont. Every time they came to see me, their arguments became more persuasive.

I was starting to feel the "itch" again. I decided to form a new company with Bob and Dave, which we ultimately named Voice Technologies Group (VTG).

First, however, I needed to fulfill my obligations and help the CIS Trustee find the best buyer for Com-Pro. Once that was accomplished, I would be free to leave and then come back to the new owner of Com-Pro to purchase everything associated with the VoiceBridge product.

That new owner turned out to be Keane and Associates of Boston. A few months passed before the deal was finalized. During that time, I was working from home to get everything organized to fund VTG. I asked Bob and Dave to stay with Com-Pro until after Keane finalized the acquisition to make sure that clients were cared for, satisfied, and that everything was moving forward.

Voice Technologies Group

Just days after Keane finalized the acquisition of Com-Pro, I opened the doors of VTG along with my new business partners, Bob Fritzinger and Dave Straitiff.

I knew this would be a challenge—I had never run a product company before. Buying back Com-Pro or starting something similar to it would have

With my VTG partners, David Straitiff and Bob Fritzinger.

been the safe play. I'd been there and done that. But I wanted a new challenge. When Dave and Bob came and talked to me about the potential hidden inside of VoiceBridge, I realized that we were really onto something.

There was an obvious initial niche to attack. Voice mail was becoming very popular and we had a ready-made solution that permitted corporations to purchase any system they wanted. Beyond that, the idea of connecting telephones and computers—something that hadn't yet been done—just seemed to be a home run for the future.

I was able to personally finance the acquisition of the VoiceBridge assets from Keane. Shares were issued to the founders (Bob, Dave and me) on November 21, 1989. As the principal founder, I held sixty percent of ownership, with the balance split between Bob and Dave. Agreements with my new partners allowed them, through sweat equity, to buy their shares over time. The first meeting of the Board occurred that evening. Although I didn't realize it at the time, VTG had taken its first step toward Silicon Valley.

This company had a future. It was time to roll up our sleeves and get to work.

It wasn't that difficult to get the business organized. I had the network of advisors that would allow us to create and organize VTG. I also had the network of people, talent, and assets that would be needed to get the company off the ground. We had a product. We had some sales and therefore a bit of revenue. We had DuPont, which was more than willing to act as a reference client and case study. And we'd done a bit of horse-trading to get our hands on old phone systems, so it wasn't going to be difficult to move beyond AT&T and into the other key teleco players.

My immediate challenge? Getting Bob and Dave organized. Neither had ever run a business, and neither understood what a startup was. Dave was only nineteen years old at the time, but he was a genius when it came to designing hardware. I put him in charge of the VoiceBridge product and then immediately hired a few people to help him. Bob was older and therefore a little more mature, but he'd never worked in this type of environment. Then

I remembered why I had hired him at Com-Pro. He could communicate, teach, and solve problems. I asked Bob to set up the services side of VTG so that we could effectively deliver products to new customers while earning their loyalty.

This gave me the structure I needed to launch the company.

To be successful, we needed to do three things very quickly. First, we needed to move beyond just AT&T and make VoiceBridge also work on Northern Telecom and Rolm. These were the "Big Three" that would give us access to about ninety percent of the U.S. market. I assigned this task to Dave.

The next thing? This was a very complicated product. We needed to find a way to support its installation once it was sold. Bob took on this task.

The rest was my job. We needed to sign every voice mail manufacturer in the world to sell VTG products. It was time for me to return to my roots and do what I do best: sell, sell, sell.

Early on, Bob Fritzinger came to me with a radical idea. The voice mail industry was two layers deep. There were companies that manufactured the products, every one of which required PBX (Private Branch Exchange – a corporate telephone switch) integration as a feature of their product. This meant they needed to buy VoiceBridge from VTG. However, every one of these manufacturers used nationwide dealer networks to install and service their products, and that was where the knowledge about VoiceBridge was really needed.

Bob suggested that we ship the product to manufacturers, and that they take credit for PBX integration and then provide service and support to the dealer network.

Initially I rejected this proposal because it would cost more. Later, it became clear that we were selling our products to companies much larger than VTG, and it might make sense if they didn't really understand everything about VoiceBridge.

It turned out to be a great strategy.

As soon as the service capability began falling into place, I immediately ran into a new challenge with the product. Having run an IT consulting firm, I was very familiar with computers and the people who manage and program them. However, I'd never owned and managed a company that built them. As soon as we were up and running, I learned the lesson that every entrepreneur needs to learn about hardware and software: engineers always want to keep making it better and better. Although the engineers wanted perfection, I needed "good enough" in order to make a profit.

I challenged Dave to solve this problem. I told him the company could upgrade the product just once, and that the upgrade needed to be good enough to last us for several years. It took a little longer than planned, but once finished, VoiceBridge-2 was the backbone of the company for many years.

With Dave focused on product and Bob focused on service, I was left to sell. Truthfully, there were aspects of VoiceBridge I didn't fully understand. It didn't matter. The product delivered a lot of value, which was easy to describe. If I needed help with technological explanations, Bob and Dave both loved jumping onto a conference call to support a sale.

Sometimes it was easy. I'd call a voice mail manufacturer and ask if they needed to integrate their voice mail with AT&T. The answer was typically yes, of course, and I had the solution and could ship it immediately. Sometimes smaller companies would sign on immediately, and I'd have a purchase order on the fax machine that night. The larger companies were a little more work. Sometimes I needed to hop on an airplane with either Bob or Dave, go to the customer's offices and manage an in-depth meeting to prove ourselves. It worked either way.

I also instilled some important values and ethics into the company during that first year. First and foremost: "Everyone sells all of the time." I expected the phones to be answered. If not, I expected calls to be returned quickly. If customers had questions, it was critical to provide answers immediately. If there was a problem, and that did happen occasionally, I demanded that we fix it quickly.

We were a high tech company in a very hot sector, but I never believed that was enough. I was determined to make the instinct to sell a part of the company's DNA. As I look back, I now realize that VTG was unusual in this regard, and that this may be a very good model for new companies.

Most startups have a vision for a product. VTG had a working product and an inventory of finished goods on Day One. Most startups have only a general idea of who their clients will be and how they'll reach them. VTG had clients under contract and a fairly good idea of the role it would play in the industry. Almost all startups begin with the technology, later graduating to the issues of marketing and sales as they work to survive. With my partners, my excellent staff, and me, we had everything in place very quickly.

In less than a year, VTG had established itself as the leading supplier of products that integrated corporate phone systems with voice mail. AT&T, Rolm, and Northern Telecom had been delivered. More phone systems were on the drawing boards. Within one year of opening the doors, we had signed on 209 of the 211 voice mail manufacturers in the U.S..

However, I wasn't satisfied with conquering just voice mail. The technology we had created had many other potential uses. Now that VTG was up, running, and profitable, I was determined to grow it beyond voice mail.

Just where to focus our attention next, however, was a very complicated question. There were many different avenues, and we simply could not attack all of them simultaneously. We needed to prioritize and figure out how to organize to enter new markets.

It was at this point that a very spirited debate began, and I encouraged it. We all knew we could do many different things with our technology, but we couldn't do all of them at once. We were going to need to make choices and sacrifices, and I wanted my entire team in agreement as we made those choices. To accomplish that, I needed to get Bob and Dave on the same page. They agreed that voice mail wasn't enough. Beyond that, they didn't agree at all.

Bob was looking at what was happening with call centers and other possible applications. He vigorously argued for expanding the capability of our products and selling them at very high margins through many of the same channels to which we already had access.

Dave wanted something quite different—the desktop. We understood how to turn a computer into a phone, and Dave wanted to go on a campaign to put our technology on every desk, replacing all telephones. It was a very glamorous objective, but also very difficult to achieve.

Bob and Dave are both strong-willed. They have egos, and they both fought for what they believed in. This kind of passion on your management team is a good thing, providing you can keep it under control.

To control the dynamic, I decided to let them "fight it out" and then I would make the decision based on the merit of their pitch to me. There was a lot at stake with this decision, and we spent many long nights debating the next best use of the technology. This was the future of the company, so the spirited and heated debates sometimes turned to arguing, but I loved the passion. I encouraged it. Pure passion is part of what drives small companies.

Eventually, I began to be persuaded by Dave.

One of these late evenings, when there may have been a bit of Schligovitz or Goldschlaeger involved, I decided to force the decision. I asked just one question: "Bob, if we go to the desktop, who do we work with?"

Dave jumped in to answer, and his answer was predictable: "Microsoft!" Bob disagreed and pointed out that VTG made hardware. Dave suggested we should be talking with Intel, which was essentially Microsoft's hardware partner at the desktop.

This made sense to me, but I really didn't know that much about Intel at the time. I asked Bob where they were. Dave had a funny look on his face. Bob answered: "408." This was good enough for me to get started. Bob and Dave had taught me that if you dialed the area code followed by 555-1212, you'd get Directory Assistance anywhere in the U.S.

As I was dialing, I looked at Dave and asked a second question: "Who's the cheese?" As in "Big Cheese." I always like to talk to the President or CEO on the first call.

"Andy Grove," Bob replied. I looked at him, smiled, and said just one thing. "He's Hungarian."

I had to badger a few people, each of whom passed me along to someone else. I wasn't getting close enough. I started to ask for Andy, speaking in Hungarian. That got me to his desk almost instantly. He gave me all the contacts I needed on the first call.

Six months later, Intel Capital made a $500,000 investment in VTG for ten percent of common stock. Simultaneously, Intel Architecture Labs licensed VTG's technology for use in desktop applications for $600,000. Now, VTG had the financing it needed to get to the next step, and it had the partner it needed to get aggressive in the market.

Just four years after selling Com-Pro, I had made it to Silicon Valley.

VTG – The Middle Years

VTG was fundamentally different from Com-Pro in some very important ways. First, VTG was founded to make a hardware product. Unlike professional services, which can be grown from sales alone, this type of business must be financed into the market. For the first time in my career, I found myself risking more than my time and reputation. I was going to need to put a significant amount of my hard-earned capital at risk.

Revenue growth at VTG did depend on the acquisition of very talented people, but it also depended on the continuous introduction of new technologies and products. This was the first time I would need to support some level of pure research, putting investor capital fully at risk. While I was able to finance the launch of the company, it would ultimately be necessary for me to convince others to join me in the effort to finance VTG's growth.

The VoiceBridge product completely transformed an industry. Before VTG, a company bought its phone system and its voice mail from the same vendor.

This frequently irritated customers because, quite often, the voice mail systems were inferior to the competition's voice mail. Very soon after VTG was founded, every company in the U.S. understood that it could buy its voice mail system from anyone, regardless of what type of phone system they owned. When the market came to this realization, very substantial investments were made to quickly devise applications and solutions that would attach to a corporate phone system. VTG was one of the three or four companies that started the Computer-Telephony and Voice-over-IP (VOIP) revolution we all now take for granted. Unlike Com-Pro, VTG could not succeed unless it launched nationally and in a very short period of time.

Finally, VTG was destined to operate with some of the largest and most powerful companies in the world. It takes discipline, dedication, great people, and great leadership to succeed at this level.

I felt up to the challenge and, as I began working with my new partners, it was increasingly obvious they were, too. We had assembled a very talented staff, with office workers reporting to Donna Boyd, who was also my personal secretary. We had a very strong sales organization led by Joe Miller, a Marketing Department led by Greg McQuay, and a Human Resources Department under the leadership of Kim Bartolotti. Our Engineering Department was led by Steve Denies and Tim Heuser and, lastly, our CFO, George Greenwood, headed up Finance and Accounting.

Our quick launch, combined with the notoriety associated with the Intel financing, quickly made VTG a highly visible company.

Which brings me to what I call the "middle years." These were characterized by technology innovation, new product introduction, access to new market opportunity, staff and management growth, and, ultimately, a crisis.

By the end of 1991, the company had relocated to new facilities and quadrupled its staff, installing all the infrastructure required to market, manufacture, sell, and support very sophisticated electronics products. Two things fueled this remarkable growth.

A party at the house with my executive staff. Greg McQuay is on the far left, and Monica Toney is on the far right holding her first child, who became part of the M.I.C.E administrative team.

First, VTG's products were unique. This meant we could charge a premium price for them. Profits from existing sales were prudently reinvested in the development of new products. And whenever a new product was introduced, it was given to all of our clients simultaneously.

Second, the investment by Intel allowed us to hire an elite team of developers faster than would have been possible had we been limited to just our sales revenues. This sounds like an ideal formula for success, and it was — for a short time.

Once it was understood that access to corporate telephone systems was made possible by VTG products and technologies, the company was inundated with opportunity. During this period, VTG accomplished a great deal.

Most importantly, VoiceBridge was made compatible with more phone systems. When a partner committed to our products, they gained access to more than 90 percent of the North American market. This was critical.

In addition to providing VoiceBridge to more than 200 voice mail manufacturers, VTG ultimately became the fourth-largest manufacturer of voice mail itself, providing full systems to manufacturers of small and mid-sized phone systems, such as Mitel and Toshiba. Few knew that VTG was doing this because the agreements were highly confidential. While this business was very attractive, it did end up causing some problems with VoiceBridge customers. The lesson to be learned was: never compete with your customers!

We ultimately learned how to use this technology on the desktop, forging partnerships with companies like Compaq Computers, Hello Direct, and Polycom. In each case, we licensed our technology and then helped the company build a custom product.

We also used and licensed the VTG technology portfolio to create strategic relationships with very powerful companies, including AT&T (Lucent), Northern Telecom (Nortel), Rolm (Siemens), Octel (Lucent), Microsoft, Intel, Dialogic (Intel), and Cisco.

There was "modularity" to this business that appealed to me. AT&T permitted VTG to enter the market, giving me something I could sell immediately. While I was doing that, the staff was busy adding support for the next phone system, which was Northern Telecom (Nortel). Once that was available, I could give it to all of our existing clients in one day. Every time my staff released support for a new phone system, it became easier to close purchase agreements with a manufacturer.

As long as I could promise a manufacturer that connecting to VoiceBridge meant they were integrating to phone systems and increasing their revenues,

I could keep their business by adding support for these new phone systems. That's how we won and held so much of the market for so long.

So we started VTG with a single product. By 1995, we were selling dozens of different products. For a small, entrepreneurial firm in Buffalo, New York, these were formidable accomplishments, but there were also some challenges. In fact, there were some serious problems building up inside the business that would eventually test us all.

Once we had a set of products that covered nearly 90 percent of the U.S.-installed base of large phone systems, the investment rationale for capturing the remaining 10 percent was hard to make. That didn't stop these small business customers—or my sales team—from asking, however. I had to impose significant financial discipline on the company so that we wouldn't spend a lot of money chasing very small opportunities.

VoiceBridge was expensive, and that was appropriate for large companies. DuPont, Boeing, American Express, John Deere, and Ford all used our product. Smaller companies bought smaller, less-expensive phone systems. As we grew, I was being pressured to deal with the low end of the market.

It's also important to note that AT&T, Northern Telecom, and Rolm all sold their own voice mail systems. As we became successful, they began to lose business to their competitors, many of which were our clients.

Although I managed to keep the company financially disciplined and focused on large opportunities, I could not prevent the big PBX manufacturers from getting anxious about VTG's success. Eventually they noticed, and this became the first crisis we faced during the middle years.

In the 1990s, the entire industry was aware that you could sign an agreement with VTG and buy access to the entire installed base of AT&T, Rolm, and Northern phones systems in North America. A migration of voice mail revenue away from these three companies was well underway, primarily due to VTG. When we were only taking voice mail revenue from the PBX manufacturers, we were largely ignored because voice mail revenue at AT&T and Northern Telecom was relatively low. It was an accommodation to make the customer happy, and they generally lost money on the sale.

However, when the industry realized that we were collaborating behind the scenes with Intel and Microsoft to transition this same technology to the desktop, allowing a PC to either complement or replace a telephone, VTG potentially threatened both voice mail and telephone revenues. The PBX manufacturers could no longer ignore us. AT&T (Lucent) was the first to act, indicating a willingness to sue to protect its intellectual property.

The threat wasn't made to VTG, however. It was Intel that received the threat. AT&T wasn't too concerned about a little company in Buffalo that might be impacting its voice mail revenue. However, they were seriously concerned that Intel might be gearing up to eliminate all telephones.

Faced with the prospect of protracted litigation with AT&T (and likely Northern Telecom and Rolm), Intel immediately dropped the desktop collaboration with us, wiping out the future royalty revenues that VTG had banked on. And, of course, at this point there was no guarantee that "The Big Three" would continue to ignore us, even in the smaller voice mail segment.

There were nights when I did not sleep. What had we gotten ourselves into? Our partner, Intel, had pulled the plug on the desktop. There was now a very real risk that VTG might have problems with AT&T, Northern Telecom, and Rolm—all multibillion dollar, global corporations.

This was not the most comfortable place to be. I knew we were going to have to fight for our business. After consulting with my partners, my management, and my Board, I decided on two courses of action.

First, I went after Intel very aggressively. We had made a deal. VTG had made plans based on that deal. They chose to back out. I didn't believe they had the right to do that at my expense. It took a little time, but eventually they accommodated my demands, paying us a reasonable portion of the anticipated royalties due under the contract. This gave us some cash and bought us some time.

Secondly, I chose to treat the potential threat from "The Big Three" as an opening to sell to them. My theory was that a deal would mitigate any threat. Bob and Dave helped me find a simple pitch. It was a little different from the standard pitch to the regular voice mail vendors, but it worked. Within six months, "The Big Three" were all clients.

At this point, VoiceBridge was used by almost everyone, and there were times when a client would get six or seven bids, with VoiceBridge included in every one of them. We were truly in the middle of it at this point.

It's a great place to be, but there was no time to celebrate because another challenge was right on the horizon.

By the mid-1990s, a significant portion of the voice mail industry, including the leading PBX manufacturers, were fully dependent on VTG. VoiceBridge was the "open standard" used to connect an application to a phone system. We had succeeded in putting most of the industry under long-term supplier agreements, achieving a near-monopoly market share in North America.

But only at the high end of the market.

The low-end of the market was much larger. For every business that owned a big phone system, there were a hundred companies that owned a small one. Our loyal customers were putting pressure on us to come up with low-end solutions. We had to act to take advantage of this opportunity.

First we moved the technology we had developed working with Intel to PC boards. Mitel was released for the low-end, followed by AT&T, Northern Telecom, and Rolm. VoiceBridge and VoiceBridge-PC became available for all our customers. This solved half of our problem.

I then asked my team to look at what it would take to build a very small voice mail system that could be put inside of a small phone system. This would eventually prove to be more controversial than the move to the desktop.

To do a good job of integrating with very small phone systems, we really needed to build an entire voice mail system. We were well positioned to do this. We had a great team that had learned everything there was to know about phone systems and voice mail. Even though Intel had cancelled the desktop project, we'd learned a lot from them about how to build computers.

In order to attack all of this opportunity very quickly, I needed to add resources, and that meant I needed to raise some money. In a fairly short period of time, VTG closed on $1.5 million in funding in exchange for twenty percent ownership (preferred). The source of the monies was local—a group of angels that included a few of the senior executives I had previously worked with at CTG. This infusion permitted the company to further expand its facilities, bring in new staff (including senior leadership), expand manufacturing capacity, and enhance marketing.

It was a bold move, but I had faith in my team.

The mistake we made was attempting to generate three new products in a very short period of time. Mitel and Toshiba went smoothly; AT&T and Merlin did not. From the very beginning, there were problems with the product—we ultimately recalled it, writing it off as a loss.

The Pressure Mounts

For me personally, there was another problem. My new investors demanded that I pledge all of my family's assets to secure their investment in VTG, including my home and bank accounts. In the end, and with encouragement from my attorney and good friend, David Roach, I decided to take that risk. But the failure of the Merlin product shook the confidence of the investors and put me in a very difficult position.

And then things got even worse. No one prepares for cancer!

VTG had expanded to occupy more than 25,000 square feet, including a specialty laboratory and manufacturing space. We had more than one hundred employees, including some of the most sophisticated hardware and software development engineers in the region. For the first time in its history, VTG revenues had exceeded $10 million, with net pre-tax profits in excess of $1 million. Record operating profits combined with an infusion of investor funds had armed the company to attack the market aggressively, and senior leadership (COO, CFO, VP of Sales, and VP of Marketing) had been recruited. The company had been reorganized into three business units. Traditional VoiceBridge products, which were performing at record levels, were given to Bob. A new business unit designed to handle small voice mail was formed. And a small team was organized by Dave to revisit the desktop. Everything was in place and well underway for the company to move to the next step.

And then I was diagnosed with prostate cancer.

I spent a considerable amount of time researching the disease. I talked with Andy Grove, the President and CEO of Intel, who had just shared with the public how he had dealt with this form of cancer. In the end, I decided to go to Barns Hospital in St. Louis for surgery and rehabilitation. I knew that I would need to spend some time away from work to get healthy and ready for the next step.

I met with my partners and members of my management team. I had heart-to-heart talks with each of them and was very gratified to learn I had everyone's support. They all knew what had to be done, and they all understood that I needed to treat getting well as my highest priority.

I knew there were a few issues building up — this is normal for a very fast-growing company. But I had confidence in my team, so I prepared to leave for St. Louis.

Part of my confidence in taking this temporary medical leave was due to a new recruit. We had recently hired a brilliant and charismatic operations executive, a Claremont graduate who had done his graduate studies under Peter Drucker. This individual joined VTG as COO just as the ill-fated Merlin was launching.

His first task was to quickly and efficiently clean things up and unfortunately, this involved some necessary layoffs. It was clear that we needed to get this failure behind us, learn from it, and move on as quickly as possible to continue our attack on the market. Once it was clear that the Merlin catastrophe was largely solved, I had the confidence to leave for St. Louis.

Other issues were brewing back at the office, however, and they erupted while I was away. First, a contract with a key client started to fall behind schedule and investor anxiety was on the rise. It then became apparent that my partner Dave was becoming increasingly dissatisfied with his role in the Company, frustrated by the sense that he had no immediate ability to advance. And, in retrospect, the COO viewed my illness as an opportunity and began his crusade to oust me from my own company.

The surgery and recovery in St. Louis did not take that long, but I was planning to spend some time relaxing and rehabilitating when I returned to Buffalo. However, the day I returned, my partner Bob dropped in to visit me at home. He told me about the issues in the office, specifically that the COO was lobbying management to oust me.

Against my doctor's advice, I went to work the next day. It was difficult because I was still catheterized. I was more than a little pissed off. I had lived up to my end of the bargain and beaten the cancer, but my staff had allowed things to get out of control.

My first task was an unannounced visit to the COO's office. On his desk was a "To Do" list. I was shocked to see "Les has to go" on this list. I was just starting to recover from the trauma of surgery and I felt slammed with another shock. My doctor had cautioned me to stay calm, to avoid trauma. This was now impossible. I did what I knew needed to be done.

I told the COO to pack his belongings and leave immediately. What I went through as a child with the Russians apparently had given me all the training I needed to face nasty situations like these. I reassumed responsibility for day-to-day operations the very next morning.

This was not how I had hoped to be welcomed back to the office, and I suspect that this unnecessary stress delayed my recovery. But we quickly cleaned up all of the issues, leaving the team intact and in place, ready for the final push. More importantly, I am happy to report that I recovered fully and I am still cancer-free.

Cancer Strikes

Learning that my Dad had prostate cancer was the worst time. I never want to go back to St. Louis again. We tried to make it fun and sightsee and laugh, but knowing the surgery was coming was horrible. We went to the arch and had dinner on the water. The one good thing on that trip was that at some point my Dad and I were alone and I was the first one to witness him touching the Mississippi River. He talked about how he dreamed of doing this when he was younger and was finally getting to touch it. I felt proud that we shared that moment. Then everything got very real. For the first time we all talked about his will and what would happen if he didn't make it through the surgery. That was the worst dinner of my life.

I remember waiting for Dad to come out of surgery. Two men had gone in at almost the same time, and the two families waited together in the waiting room. The other man received horrible news. The cancer had spread and the prognosis was very poor. I remember thinking that could have been my Dad, but thankfully it wasn't, as he still had a lot more to do. Seeing him after the surgery looking white as a ghost and so helpless was difficult. I did not know my Dad like that. He was always so strong. It was an incredibly emotional time and I am so thankful that he came through and everything turned out OK.

When we got home, I saw my Dad crying. I asked him why, and he told me he was thinking about all of the great friends he had and how concerned everyone was for him. It really meant a lot to him.

When I found out that someone he trusted tried to take advantage of him during that time, I was so angry at his business partners. It showed me that business really *can* be ruthless. There are several people in whom my Dad has trusted who have either betrayed him or taken advantage of his kindness. Even though it may have hurt him or he may have lost money or a deal, I am happy that he is trusting rather than a ruthless businessperson with no heart. That would be tough for me to swallow.

- Erika Meszaros Wayo

VTG – The Final Push

With the critical issue behind me, my next priority was to find a graceful solution for Dave. He was unhappy and there were times when this affected the rest of the management team.

VTG faced two very formidable challenges. We needed to find a way to create support for the world's leading phone systems, and then package that technology into products that made sense for our customers. The first part involved hacking together a product. The second part required building a disciplined company.

Dave found much more pleasure in the first phase, and we were all very proud of what he had contributed. As the company grew and became more structured and more disciplined, it became less and less able to accommodate every new idea Dave hatched.

In the end, Dave forced the issue by wanting a larger role. There really wasn't any way for the company to satisfy his needs in the short term without me stepping aside. He had his own ideas and wanted to run his own business. We had a heart-to-heart talk over a glass of wine. Dave poured out his soul, and I, mine. In the end, VTG repurchased his shares, giving him the capital he needed to start his own business.

This was an unhappy parting, nonetheless. Dave felt like an adopted son of mine, and this split was very painful. He was not in agreement with the plan, but he understood that business was business. This put some pressure on the company, but we ended up being a little leaner and much more focused.

There was one last thing I had to do: refinance the company. This was essential if the local investors were to realize a reasonable return on their investments, and it would allow us to move on without them. I had a strong revenue base to work with and several reliable strategic partners, but I didn't have a lot of time.

Our outside investors had notified VTG of their intent to put their shares back to VTG. This notification created a requirement to pay out nearly $3 million to reacquire that equity, due in about one year. Although VTG was able to navigate this mid-life crisis reasonably well, it was not without cost.

There was no way to redeem these shares from accounts, so I was faced with an immediate need to raise money. And the money I needed to raise was the toughest kind there is—replacement financing. When investors put money at risk in a company, they do it to grow their investment. Putting money into a company merely to buy out other shareholders is very rarely a good use of capital. I knew this, so I knew I had my work cut out for me.

At the same time, profound changes were occurring in the industry. The Internet was exploding, and corporate data networks were becoming the norm. Technology investment was shifting away from traditional telecommunications (VTG's domain) and towards this new frontier. It was already clear that corporate and worldwide data networks would eventually replace traditional telephone networks. All of these trends had to be factored in when seeking new investment.

A very high caliber operations professional was recruited into the company. This time I looked to industry rather than academia for credentials. The individual retained, Ron Kalp, was a former Raytheon executive. He had just retired after running a multi-billion dollar technology operation.

Reorganizing operations proved to be easy for Ron. VTG had just surpassed $15 million in annual revenue so, from Ron's perspective, the project was relatively small. I recognized this and asked Ron to spend a portion of his time educating middle management, passing on as much of his experience as possible. Ron was a gifted operator and a gifted educator. It wasn't long before the team was up and running.

I also promoted Bob and made him Chief Technology Officer, reporting directly to me. In addition to managing the patent and licensing portfolio, Bob was charged with revisiting the entire product line-up, reprioritizing efforts to properly position the company as the transition to Internet-based communications got underway.

Once I was confident this new team was leading the company the way I wanted it led, I got on the road to raise money.

VTG had previously worked effectively with partners to use its technology for specialty applications. While strict replacement financing can be difficult, VTG did have the ability to offer a limited license to its proprietary technology as a "premium," thereby rationalizing the investment. I drew up a short list of candidates and began talking with each one.

At the head of the list was Natural Microsystems (NMS), a Boston-based company. They manufactured the audio equipment that many of VTG's voice mail customers added to VoiceBridge products. Combining the VTG technology with the NMS audio processing was a very logical proposition.

NMS was also a logical partner for VTG. Their competitor, Dialogic, held more than an eighty-five percent share of the audio processing market, while NMS held the remainder. Enabling either of these companies under license would ultimately eliminate some VoiceBridge revenue. However, it was logical for VTG to enable the small player in the market rather than the large one. It was also likely that NMS would actually place a higher value on the VTG license as they worked to compete with Dialogic.

VTG and NMS had worked together occasionally to mutually support clients, but the primary relationships were all established at tactical and support levels. It was time for me to pick up the phone. It was time to call "the Big Cheese" and start building a relationship in anticipation of "the ask."

I spent a great deal of time building that relationship before I floated the idea of an NMS investment and partnership with VTG. I needed this deal to work. All of my personal assets were pledged as collateral to support the old investors—the ones who had put their shares to VTG. The clock was ticking and VTG wasn't able to fully redeem those investors. A failure to redeem them could conceivably put some of my personal assets at risk.

When I finally felt prepared to start the process, NMS was immediately receptive to the concept. However, the negotiations were grueling, taking nearly seven months. As the clock ticked, it became more and more stressful for me. I had to find ways to deal with that.

I found relief by exercising. I began stopping at the Jewish Community Center every morning for an hour swim. The workout was good for me, but it also gave me a calm hour away from the stress associated with getting the deal done.

I was negotiating with the CEO of a publicly traded company. I knew it wouldn't be easy. It took a long time, but it was worth it. My family's assets were no longer pledged as collateral.

While I was putting the financing in place to ensure the health of the company, Bob was busy defining what the company would be doing in the future. Nearly two dozen filings were submitted to the U.S. Patent Office in an attempt to protect projects that were under consideration. About half of them were granted and two of them are now considered "foundation patents," cited by nearly every smart phone manufacturer in the world.

An engineering effort was initiated to reduce the cost of all products. At the same time, the company funded a research effort to create a single chipset compatible with all the PBXs it supported.

We also spent a great deal of time talking with our very largest clients in an effort to understand how they thought they'd be using the Internet in the future. DuPont was revisited. Large clients like Boeing, Ford, American Express, John Deere, Southern Pacific Railroad, Motorola, and Intel were all engaged. Out of this study came a very simple plan that the company dubbed "Boards, Blades, and Pods."

"Boards" were PC boards that allowed computers to connect to phone systems to support applications like voice mail. These products were all delivered and required only support and maintenance.

"Blades" were the products for small phone systems like Toshiba. We worked with both Toshiba and Mitel to make these products useable worldwide.

"Pods" were products that used VTG technology to connect telephone systems directly to the Internet.

This very crisp "Boards, Blades, and Pods" slogan allowed us to focus on, as well as articulate, our goals when talking with customers and partners.

Much of this plan had already been delivered, with the exception of the Internet pod, which we would eventually name IPod. The Internet pod made me a little nervous, but both Ron and Bob were completely confident. They were also working very well together. I knew that if they could deliver a product and then teach me how it could be used, I'd be able to sell it.

I don't take risks just to take risks, but I am more than willing to take a calculated risk if I know the team is on the same page and the agenda is moving forward. My team convinced me that VTG was in a good position to pull this off. All of our products since inception had been designed to connect phone systems to computers. By the late 1990s, it was routine for computers in the enterprise to all be connected on a corporate network, so it was logical for VTG to start to look at how to connect PBXs to the Internet.

My team had done its homework, so I endorsed their recommendation.

Bob and just two engineers created three very quick prototypes. Nothing about these prototypes was remotely saleable, but they did prove a point. We took all three of them to the industry's largest trade show in March, 1999. This was the year that Voice over Internet Protocol (VOIP) began to emerge, and there were a number of early products being demonstrated that allowed voice to be transported over the Internet.

But there was nothing on display that allowed a phone call to be made via the Internet, and VTG appeared at this tradeshow with the IPod. It allowed a call to be started on a PBX phone and end up in a browser, including all of the functionality associated with very high-end office phones.

No one else had anything like it, and VTG was immediately invited to visit with Cisco to demonstrate what we were working on. During the demonstration, Cisco CEO John Chambers walked into the room. He played with the demo, asked a few questions, and issued an order: "Buy them."

This was the Internet go-go era, when Cisco was buying a small company nearly daily with its rapidly appreciating stock. That deal never happened, but the attention Cisco lavished on VTG, combined with the relationship I had worked to maintain with the leadership of Intel, allowed for a more logical transaction to occur just a few months later.

On February 26, 2000, I signed a plan to merge VTG with Intel. One of the requirements of the deal was that Bob and I remain on board for a year. I was named Vice President of Business Development. That allowed me to stay close to VTG to ensure a smooth transition. Intel moved into a 60,000 square foot facility in Western New York.

A year later my work at VTG was done.

I retired, leaving the company I had founded in very good hands. I took some time off with my family, did some traveling, and found new and abiding passions.

The VTG executive staff and Intel representatives during the sale of VTG to Intel in 2000.

Celebrating the sale of VTG with Bob Fritzinger.

Another dream realized following the sale of VTG.

A VTG reunion in 2011 at my house, serving my famous Hungarian Goulash.

Chris Moves On, Too

I did not feel that I was entitled to anything that I hadn't earned or learned. So, I worked hard to prove myself worthy of whatever position I was given. I spent two or three years working at the Intel-adopted VTG and decided I would leave when the right opportunity presented itself. After a few ventures with startup companies, in 2007 a good friend convinced me to join Synacor, a growing company in Buffalo.

- Christopher Meszaros

FIFTEEN | DOING BUSINESS IN HUNGARY - TAKE TWO

When I first attempted to get involved in business in Hungary, I wasn't able to devote much time to ensuring its success. I was struggling financially and building up a business, so traveling back to Hungary on a regular basis was not possible at that time. Once I "retired," I decided to take another shot at the Hungarian world of business.

A Tale of Two Countries

During a visit to Hungary in 2003, my dear friend Dr. Miklós Miskuly introduced me to István Halász, a prominent industrial builder. His company, Baustar, headquartered in Kecskemet, was responsible for building most of

the industrial parks in Tatabánya. He expressed a desire to expand his business and move beyond industrial projects. We co-founded Célorient Corporation to construct apartment buildings and rental properties. Based on our research, there was a huge demand for this type of housing in Budapest.

The partners were István Halász, CEO of Baustar, Dr. Miklós Miskuly, a private attorney, and me. We started construction in several districts within Budapest. In the Seventh and Eighth districts, which

A Christmas celebration in Kecskemet, Hungary in 2003. My business partner, István Halász, is on the far left.

were less affluent, we built apartments. These turned out to be only minimally profitable.

However, this project turned out to be a very profitable lesson on how very different Hungarian business, laws, and processes are from those I had grown accustomed to in the U.S.

For example, it was impossible to determine just how much raw materials really cost. We couldn't even verify how much was delivered at any given time unless we were physically present at each site at the time of delivery. Neither the suppliers nor the workers could be trusted. We also discovered that the laborers lacked critical skills and often failed to meet deadlines. Labor costs skyrocketed because we had not taken these factors into consideration. The entire workforce—no, the entire industry—was a disaster. Hungary proved to be an exhausting work environment.

However, another business opportunity presented itself. The vice mayor of Budapest's prestigious District One told us about a parcel of land that would soon become available. We decided to take one more crack at building apartments. We put in a bid and were awarded the contract. We decided to build a five-story apartment complex with thirty-eight units. I wound up buying the penthouse. Finally, a success!

When the last apartment was completed in 2008, I ended my involvement in the construction business in Hungary. It had proven to be too much of a headache with too little profit. But I had learned a great deal about how business is done in Hungary, and had come to understand the significant differences that exist between doing business in Hungary and doing business in the U.S.

For instance, I have found that many business leaders in Hungary systematically exclude women from business. I found this appalling, an attitude that has long since vanished from American thinking. In my experience, women often make better employees than men. I had many female employees over the years in the U.S.. I admire their hard work, honest attitude, dependability, and productivity. I am sure that the women in Hungary, given equal education and opportunities, are just as valuable.

I also found that Hungarian men who create or take over companies frequently consider themselves the boss and treat their employees as inferiors. CEOs seem to think that they diminish their status by talking to their employees, who they consider to be of a lower rank. This makes no sense to me. These are the very people who make a company successful, who bring in the profits. CEOs in the U.S. tend to surround themselves with people who are more knowledgeable than they are and provide leadership that fosters a team environment, sharing equity with key employees. I have always appreciated each of my employees, and this attitude has been an important part of my success.

God gave me the gift of leadership, but I freely admit that I am not skilled at everything. I rely on talented professionals from many fields and I believe in teamwork. Only together is it possible to have a successful company. The key is to appreciate every member of your team. You must notice everything that goes well, and then go one step further, complimenting the team on those victories. In Hungary, the CEOs speak poorly of and to their employees. How could the company possibly benefit from this?

These are some of the things that I have witnessed and learned over the decades that allow me to serve as a valuable business consultant in the U.S.. I have been able to help companies with management issues, providing strategies for building a company, handling personnel, and ensuring employee loyalty.

PART FOUR

MESZAROS INTERNATIONAL CENTER OF ENTREPRENEURSHIP (M.I.C.E.)

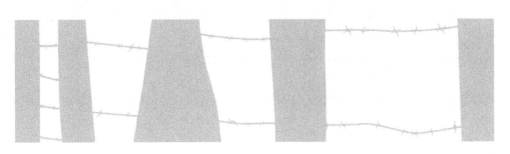

The sale of VTG to Intel in 2000, at the dawn of a new millennium, had put me in a pensive mood. In addition to my Hungarian business ventures, I consulted with a few business start-ups and served on several boards in Buffalo, where I was able to share my expertise. On the cusp of possible retirement, I began reflecting on my past and admitted to a sense of pride in my accomplishments. I felt the need to share my business expertise with young, budding entrepreneurs. I began to realize that I wanted to leave a legacy, to give back.

I decided I wanted to do this in both of my homelands. Perhaps my combined business experience in the U.S. and Hungary would enrich what I could share with youth in these very different cultures. So I founded M.I.C.E.

M.I.C.E.

No, M.I.C.E. is not a tribute to my early days at Roswell, but rather the acronym for the Meszaros International Center of Entrepreneurship, my mechanism of choice for "paying it forward."

In 2001, as a member of the Dean's Advisory Council for the University at Buffalo's School of Management, I had several conversations with professors about remaining active in the business world as a "retiree."

One of these professors, a passionate University at Buffalo (UB) educator for more than thirty years, understood both my desire to give back and contribute, as well as the demand for what I have to offer. We began working on the synopsis of an entrepreneurship program.

In 2003, that UB professor and I co-founded and I funded the Meszaros International Center of Entrepreneurship, M.I.C.E., a nonprofit 501(c)(3) organization, in partnership with the State University of New York at Buffalo School of Management. The goal of this program is to help high school juniors and seniors discover the gifts they have been given, perhaps including the innate talent to be an entrepreneur. It also builds student confidence and maturity by providing a unique and creative learning atmosphere.

The twenty-week course consists of three hours of instruction on Saturday mornings covering topics like ethical entrepreneurship, financial literacy, and business ownership. The students learn these fundamentals through content experts, guest speakers, and team projects. By the end of the course, students have received extensive training in business plan preparation and have competed as teams in a business plan competition judged by local business owners. There is also a graduation ceremony to celebrate the students' accomplishments.

Participating in M.I.C.E. can also help students excel in other academic areas by showing them "the big picture" and teaching them critical thinking skills. In the long term, this gives them the confidence to follow their dreams, regardless of the career path they choose.

I don't believe that it is possible to teach entrepreneurism; it's a spirit you must be born with. The challenge is to find out if someone has it and then to nurture it. If you can identify these individuals, it is possible to improve the odds that they will realize their potential and be successful through education, self-realization, and training. This is what the M.I.C.E. program does.

M.I.C.E. exposes students to every facet of entrepreneurship. It teaches students what they will experience as entrepreneurs, what they need to pay attention to, how to communicate, and how to dress. Armed with realistic information, they are able to determine if they really want a twenty-four/seven-day-a-week occupation, one that comes with a great deal of risk, but which also offers the possibility of great success. Students become aware that, as entrepreneurs, they will be risking their own resources, that of their investors, and perhaps even that of their families. The program helps them recognize the possibility of financial independence and prosperity while giving them the tools to achieve their goals.

M.I.C.E.

By guiding youth to realistic and attainable dreams, M.I.C.E. helps students identify their strengths and weaknesses, develop focus in their career paths, recognize their ethical responsibilities, and achieve excellence. They emerge from the program with poise, polish, and self-confidence.

– Gene Hegedus

M.I.C.E. Buffalo graduating class. Coordinator and good friend Gene Hegedus is second from the left in the second row.

Successful entrepreneurs and leaders in the corporate world are invited to guest lecture. Spending time with other entrepreneurs, especially young and energetic people, is very valuable for the students and sheer joy for me. Executives lead by example, showing that it does not matter how poor you are or where one starts. When I am in the classroom, I remind the students of the difficulties I faced as an immigrant coming into this country and I challenge them.

It is determination, the willingness to work hard, the ability to treat people equally, and commitment that leads to success.

Because we also stress the importance of stewardship and social responsibility, students graduate with a keen desire to give back to the community. Most of our graduates continue on to college and those who decide not to pursue higher education, but rather start a business, have many of the tools needed to start a successful company. All demonstrate great dedication to the program.

M.I.C.E. ultimately satisfied a debt of gratitude to America, but in 2003, the program was a moral imperative in the country of my birth.

M.I.C.E. in Hungary

Hungary spent six decades under totalitarian rule. Many personal freedoms were suppressed including the entrepreneurial instinct. Centrally planned, socialist/communist countries offer no incentives for an entrepreneur to take risks and be creative. If one does, the government owns the fruit of his or her labor. Given this backdrop and the dearth of entrepreneurial opportunities in Hungary, it was clear that this was where M.I.C.E. would be most valuable. While this program cannot make up for all of the damage done by decades of Stalinist rule, it has proven to be a good start.

For instance, in Hungary we must sometimes teach students not to follow the lead of their own parents. The practices of many Hungarian businessmen, particularly when it comes to equal treatment of men and women in the workplace, are contrary to the key concepts of teamwork and the respect for all employees that are critical to creating a successful business. The next generation of Hungarian entrepreneurs must be taught this, and M.I.C.E. has taken on this challenge.

Small business is the backbone of a free-enterprise system. While dominant brands like Apple and Google get much of the news coverage, it is really the combined efforts of thousands of smaller entities that grow an economy. So every country needs hundreds of new startups each year, but as many as 90 percent of startups in Hungary were failing. Encouraging the nation's youth to think of entrepreneurship as a career option—and to teach them how to succeed—was a palpable way for me to give back.

One of the most effective flyers we created states the purpose of M.I.C.E. quite enticingly:

Start Turning Your Dreams into Reality.
Do you dream of owning your own business someday?
Of being your own boss—in charge of making the decisions that affect your success?
The Future Starts Now.

M.I.C.E. was a hit right from the start in Hungary. The Piarista High School, Corvinus University, BKF, and high schools in both Budapest and Fonyod, all welcomed the program. More than 400 students from forty-three high schools in Hungary have now completed the M.I.C.E. program. Through a Sponsorship Fund, ten of these graduates have also visited the U.S. and learned even more about the American way of moving forward in their careers.

The first graduating class of the M.I.C.E Hungary program at the Piarista High School in Budapest in 2004.

The winners! Of the 125 students in Hungary who completed the course, these four groups won the competition. Instructor Eva Enczmann is first from left in the top row. Instructor Viki Kulcsar is last on the right in the second row.

The diverse group from 42 high schools in M.I.C.E. Hungary in 2010. Marketing Manager and Instructor Marianna Haver-Varga is second from the right in the first row.

The winning group from Hungary that came to Buffalo in 2010 to learn the American way of doing business.

M.I.C.E. in the U.S.

Building on the success experienced in Europe, we started M.I.C.E. in the U.S. in 2007. The professor and his colleagues wrote Entrepreneurship Foundation, a textbook that was published in both English and Hungarian and used in classes. To-date, nearly 300 junior and senior high school students have graduated from the Buffalo, New York M.I.C.E. program, with many receiving partial or full, financial need-based scholarships. M.I.C.E. graduates are also entitled to apply for college credit at UB for their participation in the program.

We follow M.I.C.E. students after graduation, and we're very proud to have graduated many successful students who have gone on to great and varied careers. Among them are a college basketball coach, a fashion designer, a boutique owner, a ski/snowmobile instructor, a restaurant manager, even an ecology-minded student who has made a business of raising snakes to serve as living pesticide for pest-free farms.

M.I.C.E. is "changing the world, one entrepreneur at a time."

Great credit for the success of M.I.C.E. goes to my dear friend, and colleague, Eugene Hegedus, Program and Course Coordinator since 2007. Former disciplinarian and math teacher at Calasanctius High School in Buffalo, I hold Gene in high esteem for all he has contributed to M.I.C.E. Gene visited public, private, and parochial schools and each year enrolled more students than the year before, creating amazingly diverse student groups. Tolerance and respect for all, regardless of race, creed or economic status, has been the result, a beautiful marriage of diversity and acceptance.

Thanks to the expertise of the UB professor, Gene Hegedus, instructors Scott Dixon and Heather Hartmann, as well as many guest speakers and staff, M.I.C.E. has indeed made a difference. A special thanks to Monica Toney for her relentless contributions, time, and dedication to the program's success.

M.I.C.E. instructors Scott Dixon and Heather Hartmann.

Sadly, the UB professor retired in 2012. This ended our collaboration with UB, and he is no longer a part of the M.I.C.E. team. Sincere appreciation to my partner since the inception. He was the brain behind the curriculum, a leader, teacher, and mentor. We still miss him.

The Blank Canvas | Tech Zone | Extreme Fitness
Style Me Fabulous | Buffalo Financial Group | Four Seasons Restaurant

M.I.C.E Buffalo graduates of 2007-2008.

M.I.C.E Buffalo graduates of 2009, 2010 and 2011.

Not Retired

When people ask me about my plans for retirement, I laugh at the thought. Retirement is not an option. "What's in it for you, Les?" people frequently ask. "Why don't you just relax and go play golf?"

I enjoy seeing these students gaining confidence in themselves and discovering their innate talents. So many wake up to the entrepreneurial skills that they discovered during M.I.C.E. That is when I really feel that the past twelve years of work, financial assistance, and dedication have paid off.

I intend to continue promoting and expanding M.I.C.E. for as long as I am able. I believe that there are M.I.C.E. graduates who will draw upon their experiences in the program to found companies that will transform Hungary and impact the U.S.

M.I.C.E seeks partners and sponsors who believe in educating our youth to become the future leaders. I hope that this book will inspire others to join this noble quest.

Giving Back

One of Les's greatest accomplishments is the M.I.C.E. Foundation. His goal is to give back to the next generation as much as he can about creating and running successful companies. I was lucky to meet him after he sold his second company, and we had many good conversations about his perspective on starting and building businesses and what integrity and success means to him. He has the mind of an entrepreneur that I think came about when he left his country as a young man and had to make it in the United States, relying only on himself.

At one time in our conversations, Lacibá said he wanted to transfer his knowledge and experience to as many young minds as possible. We both knew about programs that teach university post-graduate students about entrepreneurship, but they are a collection of textbook-style courses. Lacibá created a program for a younger audience, for high school students, based on his personal experience to practice and exercise having the mindset of an entrepreneur. It is a great honor for me to work alongside Lacibá as I volunteer to help in some parts of this program. I think this is his greatest accomplishment and I hope to help him carry on for many generations to come.

– Arpi Kolbe

PART FIVE

MY PERSONAL JOURNEY

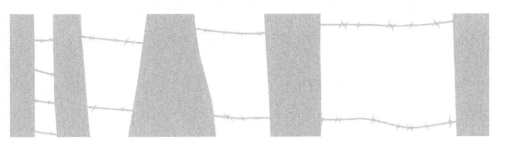

SIXTEEN | **FAMILY**

Family is such a nebulous term. Over the course of my life, I have had the honor of belonging to a multitude of families.

My first family in Hungary was by birth and bloodline, with all the genes and traditions, and included my stepmother, who I consider my own mother. I was then destined to learn other definitions of family through the devotion, love and loyalty of my close friends who I met as I began my life in America.

This family of friends started with just the six comrades with whom I escaped from Hungary to Austria. Once I arrived in America, however, my family grew by leaps and bounds. Although my roots are planted deeply in Hungarian soil, I soon found that my transplanted self flourished in American sod, blossoming into forever relationships with friends at the American-Hungarian Social Club, the Hungarian Youth Club, and eventually with the American friends who I came to know and love. My first wife, Kathy, and her family became my family, as well.

And then I started a family of my own with Donna.

Donna – My Beautiful Wife

I met Rosaria Ann Donofrio, a pretty Italian-American woman who owned a successful beauty salon, in the early 1970s. On Friday nights, Donna—short for Donofrio—and her friends and customers often went to the Depot Restaurant on Dingens Street. It was an old, converted railroad depot. One Friday evening, the CTG crew and I went out to the Depot, and the rest is, as they say, history.

Donna and I were standing next to one another in a long line and I was talking to my friends. Donna leaned over to me and said, "So, what is that accent I hear?" My immediate thought was, who is this attractive woman asking me a question?

"I'll give you three guesses. If you get it right, I'll buy you a drink." Well, she didn't get it right, so no drink. We went back to our respective tables.

As soon as the music started, I walked over to her table. "Would you care to dance?" She said yes. As we chatted, she told me that she lived in the Boulevard Towers in Amherst. I said, "Me too!"

Donna just looked at me, suspiciously, and added, "I live in Building A." "Wow! Me too!"

"Well, I live on the third floor." Her eyes now narrowed, challenging me to tell the truth for once.

"Can you believe it? I live on the third floor, too!"

She turned on her heel and walked away.

Later I asked her for another dance and she said yes. Being a European gentleman, I asked her if I could escort her home. Her reaction was instantaneous. She turned and walked away—fast!

I watched her all evening and waited until she left. I then followed her home. She was now convinced I was a stalker, but I had to prove to her that I was telling the truth. So, when I pulled up next to her in the parking lot, I asked her to not scream for the police and let me prove my honesty. When we got to the building entrance door, I opened it with my key. We then took the elevator to the third floor. When we exited, I said, "Watch, I will prove to you that I am an honest man. My apartment number is 321, and here are my keys. Go and open up the door. When it opens, you will know that I am telling you the truth."

The keys worked and Donna had to accept the coincidence and my sincerity. She went to her apartment, tired after a long day, and the evening was over.

I then moved into the next phase of my plan. I went to Donna's door the very next day, right after she had left for work, and hung a big sign that said, "Ladies, (Donna had a roommate) When you come home from work today, I will have a great authentic Hungarian meal for you. Please come for dinner."

I then went to the market and bought all the ingredients and spent the rest of the day cooking and cleaning and making a feast for those two lovely ladies.

Well, six o'clock came and went, no girls. Seven o'clock, no girls. I was getting worried. It got to be 7:45 and finally there was a knock at the door!

It was Donna. Her roommate was busy and didn't come, but Donna, who must have felt quite safe by then, was hungry, so she accepted my offer.

I had made chicken paprikash with homemade noodles, cucumber salad, and Hungarian pancake (Palacsinta) for dessert. We had a wonderful time, and that was the beginning of a relationship that would endure many decades.

We went to the movies or out dancing on most dates. I introduced her to my Hungarian friends and they welcomed her right away. They all loved her from the start, even if she wasn't Hungarian. Some of our English wasn't the best, but they all spoke English in front of her to make her feel more comfortable.

I soon met Donna's wonderful, large Italian family at one of their Sunday dinners. I am not sure what they thought of this European fellow with an accent who showed up at their home wearing pink shorts, but if it bothered them, they were quick to hide it. I met the entire family—her parents, four siblings, cousins, aunts, and uncles. They were all very welcoming, warm, and friendly. They called Donna "Sis."

The Donofrios are a very close family, full of love and, of course, lots of food. Her family all cooked well and always had an abundance of food. I was still working on my American conversation skills so it was sometimes difficult to talk about sports and other topics, but I had no problem eating her mother's delicious food and drinking her father's wine.

I was thrilled to become part of this family when Donna and I were married on September 14, 1973. I was proud to call her parent's Mom and Dad, as they always treated me like their own son. The wedding itself was not without incident, however.

A week before we took our vows, my back went out and I could barely walk. I had hurt my back a few years earlier, and every once in a while it would go out. Wouldn't you know, it had to happen the week of our wedding. I asked the priest if we could either kneel or stand during the ceremony, since changing position was so very painful.

With my lovely wife Donna on our wedding day, September 14, 1973.

With my sister Ildi and her husband Tibi on the day I married Donna.

We were married at the Hungarian church, St. Elizabeth's, by Father Skrapits, the first priest I met when I arrived in Buffalo. We had remained friends over the years and I enjoyed going to his mass on Sundays and singing in the choir. Tibi was my best man and Ildi was Donna's matron of honor. We had a beautiful, small ceremony.

When I walked into the reception at Calasanctius High School, I announced: "Yes, I am drugged up (I had been given a triple dose of cortisone and some painkillers for my back), but there is no way I am not having a drink at my own wedding reception!" Everyone had a great time.

By the following morning, however, we had already postponed our honeymoon since I could barely move. I laid flat on my back for the next three days. After being stuck in the house for days, Donna finally convinced me to take her to dinner across the street to celebrate. She sat and I stood because the pain was so excruciating. But we went out as husband and wife!

Two days later, I had to report to work. After lumbering down to my car, I discovered I had a flat tire. We could not afford the luxury of an AAA Membership at that time, so I had to ask Donna for help. She had never changed a tire in her life.

What a scene. Picture me all dressed up in a suit, not able to bend or lift, trying to instruct my new wife on how to change a flat. Amazingly, she did it! It was the time that most of our fellow building residents left for work, so we had an audience. From that day on, I was called a "male chauvinist" by all. I fell from grace, even with the group of elderly ladies who were taken with me from the day I moved into the building. It took a lot of explaining to get past that one!

After we were married, I continued my classes and finally graduated with a Bachelor of Science degree from the University of Buffalo in Business Administration. Donna continued to run her own business.

Children

We also had our first child. I was elated when I found out that Donna was pregnant. And I will never forget that day in March when Christopher was born. I was the first to hold him, and as I held him in my arms, my life changed. I flashed back to that poor, innocent baby killed by the Russian barbarian all those many years ago. The horror of what had occurred took on new depth as I held Christopher even closer. I had always wanted a child, and now, here in my arms, was the most perfect being ever. I swore to the heavens that I would do all I could to keep this baby safe forever. The blessing of that little life meant the world to me.

This was all so exciting. I had been through so many types of families, but now Donna and I were creating a wonderful family of our own. Years earlier, my father had charged me with carrying on the Meszaros name, and now I was completing this mission. Christopher Laszlo Meszaros was ushering in the next generation of the Meszaros family line.

And he was all boy! Even as an infant, he ruled the roost. When Donna and I took our first trip to the Muskoka camp in Canada with our little one, Christopher began to scream. Donna and I were helpless. We didn't know what in the world to do to get him to calm down. Nénje, who raised me before my father remarried, was visiting us from Hungary and tried her best to calm the boy down, with no

With Donna holding our son, Chris.

luck. Finally, after many attempts to console him, we gave up and decided to wrap him up and go out for a boat ride. Christopher fell fast asleep as soon as the boat left the dock. I spent the next several days of that vacation on the water, driving my son around as he slept in the bow of the motorboat.

When Christopher was two years old, Donna's family came to the house for a visit. We had a swimming pool at the time, and all of the kids except Chris were swimming. He hadn't yet learned how to swim. I said to my mother-in-law, "Mom, do you want to see your grandson swim?" And I threw Chris into the deep end of the pool, like they used to do in the old country. Of course, I was right in after him—this was the European way of teaching a child to swim. Apparently, this is not how it's done in the U.S. My mother-in-law was upset with me for a very long time.

Donna and I took Chris to Hungary in 1976, when he was three years old. It was the first visit to my homeland for both of them. The Communists were still in charge, and that made me very nervous, but it was very important that we introduce our son to my parents and family living in my homeland.

We rented a car to get to the border, and there we were stopped by the border patrol who interrogated you. They separated us, and I was so scared. I was new to foreign travel to begin with, but then, to be separated from my husband and left alone with our small child not knowing one word of the language...

They sent me to a cafe while they were investigating, but I couldn't understand a thing. It was frightening . . . nerve-wracking. I wasn't even sure I would ever see you again. The border guards went through our luggage. They opened up every one of the boxes of Pampers that we had brought for Chris and examined each and every diaper. We had brought four calculators, for gifts, and they confiscated those. But, all in all, you got us through.

– Donna Meszaros

I remember vividly the border patrol's obnoxious attitude. I was there when they pulled the luggage apart and cut up the diapers. They then found Donna's Tampax – not something they had seen before. They cut them up, sure that there was something inside. One of the guards took one and kept rapping it against the tabletop and laughing, chanting, "Tampax, Tampax, Tampax." He had no clue what these "Tampax" were.

I finally spoke up and said, "Please, there is nothing in there and we need those!" and he stopped. You see, in Hungary, even in 1976, they did not have these kinds of feminine hygiene products.

My parents were thrilled about our visit and the opportunity to meet their grandson. My father tried to keep up with Chris, but the toddler was too active for him. He nicknamed Chris the "Atomic Boy." Although my son is now a calm, relaxed, hardworking, laid-back kind of guy, and a successful businessman, his spirited side still emerges when he is watching his Buffalo sports teams. I can't imagine who he learned that from.

At the age of four, Chris spent a weekend at the home of Gloria, who was my assistant at the time. She and her husband put their three boys and Chris on ice skates. This first experience on the ice sparked a lifelong devotion to athletics. Chris played hockey, soccer, and baseball. He played on both soccer and hockey travel teams, in addition to playing on his high school teams. He was a year-round sportsman, and now enjoys golf. He also played piano for a few years.

I have vivid memories of dragging Chris out of bed at five o'clock every morning for hockey practice, driving him to the arena and watching practice before he had to get to school and I left for work. He attended Canisius High School, where he received good grades and won best sportsman awards.

Christopher left the nest and in 1995, earning a Bachelors of Science degree in Economics from the College of the Holy Cross in Worcester, Massachusetts. He then enrolled part-time at the Richard J. Wehle School of Business at Canisius College for his MBA. He continued to work at VTG while he took a class or two at a time. In 1999, he cut back to part-time work and enrolled in a one-year MBA program. He received his MBA in 2000 from Canisius College. I look at Chris, and I am reminded of my own journey to Intel.

Chris with his little sister, Erika.

Erika and Chris in Hungarian outfits.

In September, 1977, Christopher was joined by a beautiful baby sister, Erika. Donna and I could not have been happier. After all I had been through: the death of my mother, the Russian invasion of Hungary, the dangerous mine-field ridden escape to Austria, the seasickness endured leaving my homeland, and the struggle to establish myself in a new country, I now had a beautiful wife and was the father of two of the most wonderful human beings on the planet. God and my wife had been very good to me.

Erika attended St. Gregory the Great, a local Catholic elementary school, four years after Chris, and then went on to Williamsville East High School. She was also athletic and very involved in extracurricular activities such as golf, swimming, track, piano, and lacrosse. But soccer and dance were Erika's true passions. She danced from the time she was two years old, learning jazz, toe, tap, and ballet. Erika also played travel and Varsity soccer. Those were busy years, trying to balance all of the practices, games, and tournaments. My wife deserves a lot of credit for being there for both of our children.

By the time Chris and Erika were in their teens, I didn't feel the need to socialize at the American-Hungarian Social Club as I did when I was in my twenties. Neither of my children learned to speak Hungarian, but they were brought up with the traditions, the music, and the crowds of friends from Hungary, who were always a part of our life. I had to travel quite a bit for business, but when I got home, I was always happy to talk with them about their lives. I chose to spend our precious time in this way, rather than trying to teach them another language. I did, however, teach them, in Hungarian, the beautiful prayer that I had been taught as a child:

Én Istenem, Jóistenem. (My God, my dear God.)
Lecsukódik már a szemem. (As my eyes are gently closing.)

De a tiéd nyitva Atyám. (But yours are open my father.)
Amíg alszom, vigyázz ream. (As I sleep, watch over me.)
Vigyázz kedves Szüleimre. (Watch over my dear parents and my siblings.)
Meg az én Testvéreimre. (So when the sun rises again,)
Mikor a nap újra felkel (we can kiss each other)
Csókolhassuk egymást reggel. (as morning begins.)

Homecoming Tradition

I remember when I was little, after your business trips, no matter what time it was, you always came up to my bedroom to let me know you were home and to kiss me good night. We would say the Hungarian prayer together and sometimes you would even bring me a little gift from the trip that I had to wait until morning to open.

– Erika Meszaros Wayo

Wine Time

When I wasn't working and the kids weren't playing sports, we tried to do things as a family. One of those things was making wine, which has always been a welcome activity in the Meszaros household. It became one of my favorite hobbies.

Making wine in the wine cellar.

Making wine in the garage.

Chris, the young sausage-maker.

Erika learning to make wine.

Making wine was a family and friends affair. Donna's dad, Coffee, and many good friends came to the house to help with all the hard work of picking/mixing grapes. We all ate my homemade sausage and drank the previous year's wine while we washed, labeled, and corked the bottles. I sometimes let Erika and Chris taste the wine while we siphoned it from one container to another, which they loved.

We have always had a wine cellar where the wine could ferment and stay at the optimal temperature. I may have been heard saying once in my life that, "I make excellent whites and excellent reds." I don't recall, but my daughter's girlfriends often remind me of this statement. I must say . . . it is true. They were pretty good! Although my winemaking days are over, we all still love sitting around the table drinking wine.

Wine-Making Memories

During those long ago days, Les invited my friend Fred and I to join in the great fall festivals of wine- and sausage-making, presided over by Chef Meszaros. We, and various of our children, learned the sacred rituals: picking grapes, hauling them to the winery (Les' basement), crushing, pressing, adjusting sugar-levels and storing the wine-to-be in big barrels to be fermented. When the time was right, it was filter, fining, bottling, and drinking—all in Les' basement.

We bottled some 700 gallons one year, which I suspect broke a few regulations, but it was divided among four or five families. In the early years, the wines were a bit fruity, only marginally savory, but we drank it, as did my twelve-year-old son, Jonathan who, unobserved until the end of the day, was helping himself while we worked. Over time, the wines steadily improved to become truly excellent and ever present at all our gatherings.

- Dave Baer

Experiencing Life

It was important to me to give my children the opportunity to travel. Apparently, I tried to fit a lot into our travel plans. While they both feel very fortunate to have been to all of the places we went to as a family and treasure those times, they do not recall these as relaxing trips. We packed in as much as we could. More than a few times something went wrong, but we always managed to make the best of it and take in the culture. Mexico, Aruba, Paris, Switzerland, Austria, Italy, Hungary, Croatia, Finland, Bosnia, and Portugal are just some of the places we were blessed to visit as a family outside of Canada and the U.S.

We travelled to Hungary about twenty years ago once both children were finally old enough to fully appreciate my homeland. I took them to the village where I grew up, showed them my escape route, drove them to all the towns where our family lived, and spent time with all of our friends and family. It was wonderful!

We have returned to Hungary several times since then, most recently about five years ago. The six of us—Chris, Cheri, Joe, Erika, Donna, and I—attended a dear friend's wedding. What a joy! We visited family and friends in various villages and in Budapest, and we went to Aggteleki cseppkőbarlang (Aggtelek stalactite cave) and traveled through the wine regions of Tokaj, Villany, and Badacsony by Lake Balaton.

We also travelled across the U.S. and Canada for athletic events, and made some memorable trips to California, Hawaii, and Colorado. Donna and I now spend the cold winter months in Naples, Florida with a group of friends from Buffalo.

Ted, Judy, Tibi and Ildi at my 70th birthday surprise party.

The Donofrio family at Donna's parent's 50th Wedding Anniversary party.

With my father in Buffalo.

With Donna.

A special trip to Letchworth State park. Nénje, on the far right, was visiting Buffalo for the first time.

Erika's first visit to Hungary when she was six years old, with my sisters, their daughters and my parents.

Cousins: Kathy, Judy, Ted, Erika and Chris.

Donna's brothers and cousins having a few drinks at the bar in our home. From left to right: Will, Tony, Joe, Ty and Chuck.

My sister Klári with her children Bea and Akos.

Christmas Traditions

We had lots of parties at our house, and my parents still do! We either had people over or were going out all the time. Sometimes the parties were planned and sometimes they were last minute, but they always turned out great. Everyone stayed quite late, and ate, drank, argued, and laughed a lot.

Christmas has always been such a special holiday in our home. We have so many traditions...but it is anything but relaxing. Until Chris and I moved away, we spent Christmas Eve at Ildineni and Tibibasci's every year. In between all the yelling and craziness, we said a Hungarian prayer, ate our meal, and then went upstairs to wait for "Santa" to come. Ildineni rang a bell when it was OK to come downstairs. Then we would sing a few Hungarian songs as my dad played the keyboard. Finally, we all went to midnight mass, and then got a few hours of sleep.

On Christmas morning, my dad woke us up by playing the piano or putting Christmas music on. Once we were old enough, we had mimosas, breakfast and then opened presents. That was the quiet part of the day. Then we went to the Donofrio side of the family for a few hours. In the late afternoon, the Hungarian side of the family and many friends came over to our house bringing with them whoever was visiting or didn't have anywhere to go for the holidays. My mom and I always had extra gifts wrapped and waiting for whatever stranger-turned-friend came over so they would have something to open.

For many years, we sang Christmas carols. The best part was when the Hungarians tried to sing the Twelve Days of Christmas. We kids would try so hard to organize them into groups and explain how it worked, but with their accents and unwillingness to follow directions, we rarely made it through. It cracks me up every time I think about it. I vividly remember my dad laughing until he cried.

– Erika Meszaros Wayo

We have always been a family that enjoys getting together with friends and family. We are known for having parties, inviting guests, and spending our holidays together. We know how to live and enjoy the good life.

The Christmas tradition in the Meszaros home has been to invite our friends without relatives and immediate family into our home on Christmas day. While Donna and the children go to visit the Italian side of the family for a few hours, I usually stay home to cook a Hungarian meal for our dinner guests.

Cultural Challenges

Donna and I have had a wonderful life together, although like most couples, we have weathered many storms, both literally and figuratively. My many absences due to work created a lot of stress and controversy. However, those trying times stimulated dialogue about important issues in our marriage and ultimately made us stronger. So, like anything worthwhile in life, we have had to work at our marriage. After more than forty-two years, we have shared many joys, have found a lot of common ground, and enjoyed a lot of love.

Our cultural differences created something of a barrier right from the start. For instance, parenting styles were most definitely opposites. I was strict, especially about good grades and cleaning all the food off their plates. I wanted to raise the children the way I had been raised, right or wrong. Donna, on the other hand, was lenient; that is how she grew up. Her way of punishing the children was, "Wait until your father gets home!" So I often had to be the bad guy, and the children sometimes resented me.

Gratitude

Because of you, I have a fantastic life. I can do whatever I want, go wherever I want, and travel. I have my beautiful children and a lovely home. I have met many interesting people and made many great friends. But, I have also fought for this marriage and fought to remain strong within myself. You are a determined man, full of passion for life, and that can sometimes be overwhelming.

Sometimes I have feared that the yelling and shouting were detrimental to the children, but they have become very loving individuals, strong and honest. It has been a challenge to live in the shadow of such a charismatic man, but I am proud to say that I have carved out a wonderful life for myself.

Still, so much of that life is centered around you. You introduced me to Europe, among other places, and I am so grateful for all I have seen of this planet.

– *Donna Meszaros*

In my defense, Donna was often complimented for the way that our children always finished their meals when they visited their friends' homes.

Interestingly, Donna has never complimented me on helping achieve this, but at least she has passed the compliments along to me.

Our children never did drugs or abused alcohol, at least not in front of us. I was a vigilant father. I even tested to make sure they could be trusted. Whenever they were going to have a party at the house, I etched the liquor bottles. I also invested in a measuring device for the percentage of alcohol in case they tried to replace the liquor with water. I am happy to report that they never disappointed me.

I feel such gratitude that I was able to provide my family with a lifestyle that included many journeys to so many different lands. We have been able to learn a great deal about diverse cultures. Donna has beeen an integral part of building my businesses, for which I am also very grateful. She is one of the most loving, supportive and kind people I know, and is a wonderful mother and friend to our children. Donna and I really grew up together, and both worked very hard to build our lives.

Sometimes the cultural differences, coupled with my accent and the language barrier, have been a real pain in the neck. At first, it was the fact that I felt excluded from the banter among my co-workers because I couldn't converse about American sports and politics. Then, and even more seriously, I remember being discriminated against during a job interview in the south.

I was working at Roswell Park when I heard about an opportunity to work in a hospital lab; I think it was in Richmond, Virginia. I went for the interview and the staff seemed to be very pleased with me. At one point, a German doctor took me aside and cautioned me about a problem I was bound to encounter there. He strongly suggested that, due to the prejudices of many of the citizens and staff there, I might want to stay away from the job. I took his advice to heart.

Later, as I was building my business, I encountered bias and prejudice that added yet another challenge. I never let these things stop me. I simply kept moving forward because I was determined to achieve my dream. I realized and appreciated the opportunity that was in front of me in this country.

The children survived the cultural differences, and perhaps even benefitted from the balanced parenting that these ultimately produced. We share our love and devotion to Christopher and Erika, who have both grown into wonderful adults.

'American Things'

There were times when I was younger when I wished you understood 'American Things' better. I don't know why or exactly when, but I remember saying to you once, when I was very little, "Why can't you just be like other American dads?" I don't even know what I meant by it, and it bothers me now that I could have said that to you. I think it was because I felt like sometimes I didn't understand you, and in return, that you didn't understand me.

Sadly, I didn't appreciate your language and heritage when I was young. I am so grateful that once I was a little older, I was able to learn more about your struggles, our family, and appreciate the differences. I cherish the times we have gone to Hungary and for all you have taught us because of what you came from. So, now, I want to say thank you for the amazing life you have given all of us.

– Erika Meszaros Wayo

A father and son toast.

Family portrait.

A mother and daughter portrait.

From Children to Grown-Ups

During the VTG years, Chris met one of my employees. Cheri started at VTG as my secretary and eventually worked her way up to become one of the top VTG salespersons. She is a vibrant person, a go-getter, and very personable. Everyone liked her, and she was always the life of the party at the VTG get-togethers.

Chris and Cheri hit it off and began dating. Initially, they kept their relationship from us, but Donna and I were getting concerned. We asked Chris why he wasn't dating or seeing anyone, and he finally admitted that he was seeing Cheri. He hadn't told us about their relationship because he feared our reaction to their age difference and the fact that Cheri had been married previously and had two daughters.

However, both Donna and I were thrilled. We stopped worrying about Chris, knowing he was happy in a loving relationship. Chris and Cheri recently bought a house together, where they live with their beloved dog Murphy. His mother and I are happy that they have stayed close to home.

Erika chose to attend the University of Colorado at Boulder. She graduated in 1999 with a B.S. in Business Administration and Human Resources and then enrolled

Chris and Cheri with their dog, Murphy.

in Hawaii Pacific University in Honolulu, where she completed an MA in Organizational Change and Development. Erika now works in human resources, specializing in organizational development and talent management.

Erika met Joseph Wayo while working at Wild Oats in Boulder in 2005. After a few years of friendship, they started dating after Joe left a Jim Kelly Football card on her desk for Valentine's Day. Joe graduated from Ball State University in 2002 with a Bachelors of Fine Arts, specializing in Graphic Design and Marketing.

Erika and Joe were married in 2013, at the beautiful St. Joseph's Cathedral in downtown Buffalo. The reception was held at the newly restored Statler Hotel. My

With Donna, Erika, Joe, Cheri, Chris and Murphy, Christmas 2010.

long-time dream of walking my daughter down the aisle came true, and I had the honor of singing the *Ave Maria* at the church and other songs at the reception. I felt like the luckiest father on earth.

I prayed for weeks that I would not lose my voice and be healthy for this once-in-a-lifetime event. There were more than 200 guests at the wedding. A gypsy band from Toronto played during the cocktail hour, while *pálinka* (moonshine) and *pogacsa*'s (salty biscuits) were served. It was like a scene from a movie—gypsy music, friends, and Hungarian treats—nothing but the best for my daughter. We danced to music by Big City Horns, an eight-person band, until way past midnight.

Father and Son-in-Law

It means the world to me that my parents have embraced Joe and his family and consider him a son. Joe happens to be partially Hungarian, which I'm sure has nothing to do with this . . . Joe's dad and my dad were singing an old Hungarian song within ten minutes of meeting each other, quickly followed by pálinka shots and Hungarian sausage. The two families get along very well!

Joe and my dad have had some good heart-to-heart talks and enjoy discussing politics, life, and sports. Joe helps my dad with any computer or smart phone problems—he is the most patient of us all with him. They Skype or talk on the phone from time-to-time, sometimes just to say hi and have a shot. Joe loves watching my dad order his drink—a perfect vodka manhattan. He tests almost every bartender to make sure they get it right. He has definitely sent some back over the years. His highest compliment is, "Tell the bartender he/she made a fairly good drink."

– Erika Meszaros Wayo

Joe currently works as a marketing specialist and also does website and graphic design work. In fact, my very talented son-in-law designed the graphic representation of my escape from Hungary featured on the cover of this book.

Erika recently came home to Buffalo for the annual 2015 Ride for Roswell. Chris, Cheri, Erika, some cousins and friends, and I rode to remember the loved ones we have lost to cancer, to celebrate those who have survived, and to fight for our loved ones who are currently battling cancer. It was a cold, rainy day, but it was very special to ride with my family along the Niagara River. This may have been the first time that we had all ridden bikes together.

Reflections

It is hard to put almost forty years of memories into a paragraph. So here are some thoughts about my dad in a few paragraphs:

He is one of the most unique, courageous, complex, stubborn, determined, generous, passionate, and loving people I know. He has brains, courage, and a lot of heart! He talks to strangers no matter where we go and asks a ton of questions. However, he is not one for small talk or chitchat. It drives him crazy when we don't make decisions immediately. One of his mottos is, "why wait until tomorrow when you can do it today." No matter how many places he travels to, he is still amazed at what the world has to offer and how beautiful the scenery is along the way.

His happy places are when he is swimming, cooking, or singing. He may not be the most patient man and we may not always agree, but he is the kind of dad who comes into the airport every time I arrive home and is waiting for me with open arms no matter how old I am. He is emotional and sensitive and I never have to wonder how much I mean to him or how much he loves me because he shows me and tells me every day. I admire his energy and determination.

There are not too many people like my dad. Everything he has accomplished, what he does for the M.I.C.E. program students, and how he lives, are truly inspiring. When my parents are not bickering, they are really cute together. They are both excellent dancers and when they laugh together it is pure and genuine. I love watching them hold hands when they walk together, and they are always up for an adventure. They are very social and have a lot of fun together. They have both contributed to the other's success in their own ways, and they depend on each other. None of us is perfect, but they are simply the best parents and friends anyone could ask for. I hope they both know how much I love them, how grateful and thankful I am to both of them, and how truly special they are to me.

– Erika Meszaros Wayo

First high school dance.

Dancing up a storm.

New Year's Eve at the Transit Valley Country Club.

Erika and Joe on their wedding day.

Erika on her wedding day.

A father-daughter wedding day hug.

Me, Donna, Erika, Joe, Joan and Mike Wayo.

Walking Erika down the aisle after singing the Ave Maria from the balcony.

Cheri, Chris, Erika, Joe, Donna, and Me.

Singing with the Hungarian Gypsy band at the reception at the Statler in Buffalo, NY.

Erika and Joe with the Donofrio cousins.

Photos courtesy of Neal Urban Studio

SEVENTEEN | **EXTENDED FAMILY**

I have mentored many young people over the years, and although they are not my biological children, most have become members of our extended family. Our home became their home away from home, just like those I enjoyed when I first moved to this country.

Ivan Harangozo was one of these youngsters. His parents lived in New York City. Ivan showed up at my front door one day and said, "You probably do not know me, but you do know my parents." He was right. I didn't know him, but his face looked familiar. His father and I grew up as neighbors in Szentpéterfa. Ivan was attending the University at Buffalo when we met, and he quickly became part of the family, attending many parties and spending holidays

With Ivan Harangozo and his family.

with us. He is currently a successful doctor in Virginia, and we remain close to this day with him and his family.

I met Peter Palkovic through George, a good friend in Hungary. Peter was undecided as to what he wanted to do with his life, so I suggested that he come to the U.S. to enroll in one of the programs run by my friend, Dr. Peter Forgach. This program allows Hungarian graduates to get their MBA in Catholic colleges throughout the City of Buffalo. Peter enrolled and finished at the top of his class. He eventually went back to Hungary, secured a good job, and started a family. Peter was married a few years ago and my family attended his wedding in Hungary.

With Donna and Peter Palkovic.

Peter and Nikolett Palkovic's wedding in Hungary, May 2010.

Open House

All our lives we had visitors staying with us and showing up for different occasions. Our dad would literally take in anyone, mostly Hungarians, and treat them with kindness, offer advice, and treat them as part of the family. Some came and went in a few days, weeks, or months, while others became part of our life and members of the family. Soon after Arpi showed up at our house, he became part of our family and is like our brother.

– Erika Meszaros Wayo

Celebrating my 75th birthday with young members of my extended family.

Arpi Kolbe contacted me out of the blue in the spring of 1998 after a woman he met on the farm where he worked gave him my name. She had worked for me and felt that, because I was Hungarian, I could somehow help Arpi. He called and we began chatting. I invited him over to get to know him better and there was an instant connection. I became his advisor, mentor, and then friend. Our families are still very close and I often call him my third child.

Like a Father to Me

At our first meeting in person, I already looked up to Les as a father figure because of the way he welcomed me into his home. He told me his incredible story and asked me about my situation and future plans. Right away he gave me guidance and offered his help in order to better understand this country and how to be successful here. This was an amazing time for me. He welcomed me and introduced me to his family. From then on, Les invited me to all their family gatherings and holidays. These were all very special times for me since I was far away from my real family in a different country, but Les' family always made me feel right at home.

The summer of 1999 was another memorable time for me because Les bought an airplane ticket for me to visit my parents in Hungary. This was the first time I returned home after almost three years. I cannot even describe how happy my parents and I were to see each other again.

As we became closer, Les became "Lacibá" to me. Lacibá is very passionate about life. He loves food and wine and is an excellent cook, and he loves to sing beautiful Hungarian songs. He works hard and he is very generous. He helped me through the last year of my University studies and set me up with a car and my first real job after I graduated in the spring of 2002.

Before I graduated, Les and Donna offered me their sponsorship to be baptized at their Catholic Church in Williamsville. This was a great honor. When we were growing up in Hungary, baptism and going to church regularly were not considered normal. I remember one night, Les and I had a conversation about how a man is really defined—family, career, personality, and heritage. Then Lacibá told me that you can be successful or lose it all in life, but there is one thing that can never be lost and truly defines one, and that is Faith. He explained how important faith and religion are in his everyday life.

Donna came with me once a week to Bible study group for many months, and on March 31, 2002, Easter Sunday, I had my baptism and confirmation at Saint Gregory the Great in Buffalo. My parents traveled from Hungary for my baptism and at the same time, I was graduating with my Bachelor of Science degree from the University of Buffalo.

This was the first time my parents had ever traveled so far. It was also the first time in my life that I had felt a sense of accomplishment and was able to share it with my parents in the company of Lacibá and his family. They were all very proud of me and I was very happy that they were able to meet and spend time together. My parents stayed at Lacibá and Donna's home during their visit and were treated like family. They sang Hungarian songs together into the nights that just perfectly rounded out how their friendship evolved right before my eyes.

Arpi's christening at St. Gregory the Great Church. Chris, me and Donna with Arpi and his parents, Mary and Arpad Kolbe.

I have countless more great memories with Lacibá and hope to have many more! He is a one-of-a-kind great man with endless accomplishments. I witnessed him many times making a huge difference in many people's lives and he has truly made a positive impact on my life, as well. And for that, I am forever grateful to him and his family.

– Arpi Kolbe

Fun With Friends

Donna and I have gone on many amazing trips with good friends. We have great memories from the Caribbean, Europe, Dubai, Abu Dhabi, and Greece. And we have recently taken up cruising.

With Donna in the Caribbean. We vacationed in Montserrat with good friends the Baers and the Stadards.

Fun in St. Martin with Dave Baer (center) and Fred Stadard.

We were privileged to travel around the globe with Paul Finnegan's Group to attend Voicemail Association (VMA) conferences. "The VMA meeting in Greece stands out in our memories, since Les injured himself climbing the rocks along the beach and had to be hospitalized," recalls Finnegan. This memory triggered another one for Donna.

"The trip to Portugal was one of the most meaningful trips I have ever taken," says Donna. "I was thrilled because I knew the Shrine of Our Lady of Fatima was there. This was the first location I visited where the Blessed Mother had appeared. I was so touched by all the trouble you went to making sure I got to the site. I am honored to say that, over the years, I eventually also visited the shrines in Lourdes and Bosnia."

We travelled to Finland, too. " It's the cleanest country I have ever seen," exclaims Donna. "We were there with several other couples, and I mentioned how close we were to Russia and how much I wanted to see that country. It was in the late 1990s. The political situation was not stable and it was a tad dangerous for Americans to enter Russia. Somehow, even though you said it was impossible, you got visas for all six of us. Before long we were in St. Petersburg, visiting places like the State Hermitage Museum, one of the world's largest art museums with more than three million pieces of art."

Talk about risks . . . I left the group shortly after I understood the depth of Donna's desire to see Russia to figure out a way to get visas for all of us. Knowing European life, I knew where to head: the train station. So off I went.

Then came the real discernment task. I had to observe the behavior of all the men and women in the station, how they walked, how they talked, what kind of clothes they wore, and most of all, how guilty they looked. Who had a "black market expression?"

Within a couple of hours, I had found my mark. I kept an eye on him until, after whispering a little prayer, I approached him. "Say, sir, you look like a very intelligent and knowledgeable man. I am wondering if you can steer me to the right place or the right person to get some visas for six Americans who want to visit Russia." Then I held my breath. He was either going to help me or hurt me . . . I waited to see which.

He looked right, then left, and finally in a soft tone said, "Follow me, I think I know just how to help you."

I followed this stranger. He took me into a nearby vacant room. I told him what I wanted to do, the city we wanted to visit, the number of days away, and so forth. "I can do this," he said. "I need a down payment, and within three days, you will have the necessary papers. Meet me here at 9 o'clock tomorrow morning with the names and addresses of all six people and the money."

There I was, the very next morning, with the money and a list of names and addresses to give him. And, yes, he showed up! He then told me where to meet him two days later, and instructed me to bring the rest of the cash.

I returned to the hotel and told the others what I had done. Some were visibly nervous, some were fine with the plan, and Donna was not so sure about the whole thing anymore. I told them all not to worry. Even though it was a sizable outlay, if the man did not live up to his end of the bargain and the money was lost, I would take care of it myself. They were safe.

Two days later, I entered the train station and, thankfully, there he was! I walked up to him. He whispered, "You ready? Have you got the cash?" He then held out six visas and let me examine them. Not being an expert, I hoped that they were realistic enough. I took the visas, handed him the cash, and we parted ways.

The next day, we got on the train and traveled across Finland to the border where, without appearing too nervous, we were accepted with our visas into Russia. I guess there is honor among thieves.

Who Vacations at a Brothel?

Good friends George and Marilyn Greenwood recently reminisced about our travels. I started the trip down memory lane with a tease. "If not for me, your matchmaker, you two would never have met!"

"Yes, we always tell the story about how we met in your living room back in November, 1984," Marilyn said. "And we do credit you with being our matchmaker."

George chimed in immediately, "Hey, how about the Great Dominican Caper?" At George's mere mention, we all broke up laughing. We had cleverly made reservations for a one-night stay at a very expensive hotel near the airport in Santo Domingo for the last night of our vacation. The idea was to take full advantage of the six nights at the south shore, all-inclusive resort. But then, the plan changed.

"Remember how we found out about the new place? We were at that delicious German Buffet when we saw some quaint little guesthouses near the restaurant. We asked what they were. The owner said, 'Oh, those are places for you to stay, but you only pay ten dollars a night per person,' recalled Marilyn.

"Les, we have had thirty years of excellent adventures, but this one adventure beats them all," said George.

Vacationing in Mexico with Marilynn and George Greenwood.

"We should have known, though, folks, when the desk clerk told us, very firmly, 'Do not leave your rooms after nine o'clock. If you need anything at all, just call the front desk, and we will bring it to you.' Um, don't you think we should have suspected something?" Marilyn said.

Donna added, "I was not really happy when he said, 'At nine o'clock we let the guard dogs loose, so it's dangerous to leave your room.'"

"We must have been crazy," said Marilyn. "All night long, I kept hearing motorcycles pulling in and then pulling out. Those guard dogs were barking off and on all night, too."

"Yes, but did we not have a great time and get away cheaply?" I had to defend myself. "Ten dollars a night versus the two hundred dollars-plus a night at the Continental in Santo Domingo?"

Well, we did have a nice time there. But when we got on the airplane the next day to head home, a man seated near us overheard us reminiscing. He suddenly lit up and said, "Oh, you mean the brothel?"

We nearly fainted! We had just spent the night in a Dominican whorehouse! I doubt many people can put that in their travel log.

"Les, I love that over all these years that, although you've made so many new and fascinating friends, you've never forgotten the old ones." Marilyn ended the evening with that comment, and I will never forget it.

The Super Marathon

Among other activities, I am also an avid bicyclist. In 2003, my wife and I, along with eight of our friends, entered a Super Marathon in Hungary. The five-day race covered 425 kilometers (about 261 miles), starting in Vienna, Austria and ending up in Budapest, Hungary. I bike regularly; weather permitting, but I had never ridden a bicycle that many miles for so many days in a row. It was a huge challenge.

The event began as an international running marathon in Hungary directed for many years by my friend, Sándor Nagy. I met Sándor and his wife, Erizsi, in 1996, when Buffalo hosted the Athletic World Championships for Veterans. There were about forty Hungarian participants. Their leader, Sándor, came for an advance visit to get the event organized. Unbelievably, we met because Erizsi read through the Buffalo phone book and called anyone with a Hungarian name. She was looking for someone to help them with transportation, housing, and to find ways to keep the team entertained during their stay. I was the last one she called and this was right up my alley. I was happy to help support the team and we became great friends from the experience.

In 2003, I suggested that Sándor expand his Super Marathon event to include biking and rollerblading, which he did. Then I needed to put my money where my mouth was and provide him with a team from the U.S. Where would I get a team of friends who would, or even could, bike 261 miles?

I spread the word just within our close circle of friends. "Who wants to go on an adventure?" I was shocked. Eight of our dear friends were anxious to hop over to Europe to go for a bike ride! Honestly, I think they were enticed by the promise of Hungarian food, wine, and *pálinka* (moonshine).

Team USA

Les was planning a bike trip from Vienna, Austria to Budapest, Hungary about ten years ago called the 'Super Marathon' and he was putting together a team from the U.S. to accompany him and his wife on this trip. I was excited about the trip but my wife was not interested in going, so I did not respond to any of Les' requests for traveling companions. However, about a month before the trip was to occur, Les and Donna were at our house for dinner with two other couples, including Tony and Mary Martino, who were going to accompany Les and Donna on this trip. They talked so enthusiastically about the trip that my wife and I decided that night to go with them.

So we traveled to Hungary with Les and Donna, spent about ten days together, including the five or six day bike trip along the Danube in Austria and through the mountains of Hungary, finally ending up in Budapest, where a large ceremony took place. Les was very proud to be the first rider to cross the finish line in his native Budapest, followed by his contingent of U.S. bike riders.

One evening we were at a restaurant in Obuda, on the North side of the Danube River, enjoying a traditional Hungarian dinner with Hungarian music. Les has a phenomenal singing voice, and was singing songs in Hungarian. After what was probably too much wine, most of us were trying to walk around balancing full wine glasses on our heads as we enjoyed the music and the camaraderie.

On this particular trip, Les had taken care of all of the arrangements including renting the bikes and a sag wagon for those who had trouble riding at any particular time. He also arranged to have a masseuse available each evening so that anyone who felt sore from the day's ride could have a massage to alleviate some of the aches and pains.

We also spent a night at the Olympic training facility for Hungarian athletes in the town of Tata. It was quite the experience staying at their training facility.

– Dale Demyanick

We Made It

I have vivid memories of being cold! It was, after all, October when we started this amazing experience. Not just cold, but cold and rainy, too, some days. I had pictured a nice ride through the countryside, up hills and down, alongside meadows . . . but no, we rode up and down mountains! However, I discovered a huge secret to survival: pick out a cyclist and stay right behind him. And it worked. We started in Vienna, and that was the last time I biked anywhere near Les. He stayed ahead of us all, with Peter Matheisz and László Egger from Boston right with him. It was awesome! In the end, we rode the red carpet right into Heroes' Square in Budapest, where the race ended!

– Tony Martino

Revisiting the river between Austria and Hungary during the Supermarathon.

With Donna during the Supermarathon in Hungary in 2003.

The Supermarathon bike crew in Budapest in 2003. From left to right: Tour guide, Peter Matheisz, Peter Forgach, Dale Demyanick, Patty Demyanick, Terry Wegman, Tony Martino, me, Laszlo Egger, Donna Meszaros, Susan Martino Burke, Mary Martino.

The Team recovers at the PAX Hotel following the Supermarathon. From left to right: Peter Matheisz, Terry Wegman, Patti Demyanick, Dale Demyanick, Mary Martino, me, Susan Martino Burke, Laszlo Egger, Donna Meszaros, Tony Martino.

I can honestly say that this trip was one of the best I have ever taken. Seeing some of my colleagues struggling somewhat to make the distance, I empathized with them. But I could only admire the competitiveness that drove us to push and push and not fall behind. None of us had ever biked this distance before, but somehow we all made it. When, for the first time in her life, Donna biked sixty-five miles on the first day, I couldn't congratulate her enough.

Just before crossing the finish line in Budapest, I put an American and a Hungarian flag on each bike. As a united team, we rode in to Heroes' Square together. The TV stations went wild. "Here come the Americans, here come the Americans!" I felt like a million bucks. I was trembling inside and thanking God for giving me the strength to do this. The media singled me out and interviewed me about my past, my unique background as a return escapee. It was a great time for all of us, and I thank my friends who joined in and added to this unforgettable event in my life.

REFLECTIONS

I was sixteen years old when I fled my beloved Hungary, rejecting the abuse and abomination of the communist regime. Let me be clear: I did not leave Hungary because I wanted to. Hungary was my beautiful homeland, the place of my childhood. My family ties will forever be grounded in that sacred soil. No, it was not disdain for my birthplace. I left because I craved freedom and a place where I could reach for my dreams. For that reason, in August 17, 1955, I started my journey to a new world, to America, my second home.

I believe that we shape our own lives. But pivotal to success is awareness of the guidance of God. From being a refugee to becoming a self-sufficient individual was an intriguing process for me. There must be a reason, a formula, for turning survival into thriving, I thought. I needed to understand it and to share it.

So, through an intense personal assessment process, I began to appreciate my life and all it has entailed, as a healthy sense of gratitude and pride arose in me. Gratitude for God's ever-present help, and pride that, after all of the traumas and obstacles that have presented themselves throughout my life, I have remained a functioning, productive, and loving human being. After all, how many people have resigned themselves to poverty and victimization after witnessing, firsthand, the horrors of barbaric treatment? How many have simply gone mad?

Now, at the end of my entrepreneurial career, this review of my life has helped me better understand what my existence has meant.

I confess, I have sometimes struggled, wondering just where my allegiance lies, only to discover that I have made room in my heart for two loves: Hungary and the United States of America. And now I have found the perfect vehicle to express this dual love. M.I.C.E. reconciles this emotional tug-of-war by allowing me to give to the youth of both countries. Thanks to M.I.C.E., I am still not officially "retired" and I hope never to be. There are young adults out there who need my support and encouragement.

At the 2002 Hungarian World Conference in Balaton.

Until now, I have kept silent about my life. But now there is a force driving me to share my knowledge and experience. I want my family and friends to know all the hidden tales, all the buried traumas, and to know why I feel this need to gain a better understanding of myself. Documenting how I moved through war, betrayal, abandonment, homesickness, and prejudice has been cathartic. Discovering the power of reveling in songs, in socializing, and in the growth I experienced through my constant pursuit of higher education has been enlightening. With the hope of inspiring someone else to never give up, I have opted to tell my story.

While intended to be instructive, my book is at times sad. Other times, it is brimming with cheerful memories. Sometimes it is biased because it is filled with people and events that are important to me; without them, the story of my life would not be complete.

It is with love that I offer this book to every one of you. I hope you will gain some inspiration from the development of my career and the deep feelings I have for my family and friends. Perhaps you will come to understand what it means to live with two homes in your heart.

Enjoy!
Laszlo Meszaros

ACKNOWLEDGEMENTS

While this book tells my story, it could not have been written and published without the help of several very important people.

Nancy Jo Eckerson worked tirelessly to help make my words tell the stories I needed to tell. I am grateful for her patience and kind assistance.

My daughter Erika spent many hours poring over the text and sorting through pictures, bringing insights only a family member can to the task. Without her help, this would not be the compelling tale it has come to be.

My son-in-law Joe Wayo, creative artist and graphic designer, captured perfectly my escape from Hungary. I thank him for the haunting illustration on the cover that depicts the fear and despair that drove me to flee to America.

I especially thank my wife Donna for the support she has shown for me and for this project. Without her, I would not be who I am today.

And since this is the story of my life, I would be remiss were I to neglect to mention the many friends who have played roles in this remarkable story.

My Circle of Friends

The first thing that one must do to gain a true friend is to be one to yourself. I am proud to say that I have learned to love myself. Not in a conceited way, but by having a healthy respect for myself. I believe that when you love yourself, you are able to love others to an even deeper degree. While researching this book, I found many lists of characteristics of a good friend.

The true friends are those who accept you as you are. They are dependable, honest, supportive, and giving. They listen to you, and are there for you. True friends give you space. And most of all, they are happy for you when you succeed.

All of you, my friends, possess these traits. As an entrepreneur from birth, I understand that anything worthwhile takes time to create. This also applies to "true friends." True friendships do not blossom overnight; they must be built, experience-by-experience, interaction by interaction. Finding a true friend and being one in return are the best investments one can ever make. For me, this is the truth.

More than Fifty Years of Friendships

Louie (Lajos) and Mary Nemeth – Helloooo Louie! My friend since the escape. With his laid-back personality, he is always adding something funny or important to the conversations. It's a wonder, though, with our longevity, how he never adopted my outgoing, big mouth. Mary is a good-hearted woman who keeps us on our toes, especially when it comes to our faith and religion.

Peter and Judy Matheisz – My former in-laws who I still consider my family. They are great travel partners and we spend Christmas night and many other celebrations together. Judy is our voice of reason and the captain navigator on our adventures. Peter has been known to dance on a tabletop a time or two, and he and Judy are like Fred and Ginger when they dance together.

Ted (Tivadar) and Ildi (my sister and brother-in-law) – Ted is the life of the party and the center of attention. And that laugh that we love! Ildi likes to shoosh him and let others have their time in the limelight. My sister is the most understanding woman. She loves to reminisce about the past. She has the best heart of anyone I have ever met.

Gene (Jeno) and Maria Hegedus – Gene, the joker, should stick to his poetry. In later years, Gene was a significant contributor to the success of M.I.C.E. When his wonderful wife Maria is not keeping Gene in line, she spends her time cooking and is a great chef. She is one of my "rivals" in the kitchen and made all of the Hungarian desserts for my daughter's wedding.

Vince (Vincent) and Klári Somogyi – The youngsters of the group. Vince speaks the mother tongue a lot and Klári reminds him from time to time to speak in English. Vince is hardworking and tells it the way it is. Klári is also a great cook and makes wonderful Hungarian desserts. We have spent many Thanksgivings and Christmases together and have developed such a great friendship. I am Godfather to their son, Vince.

Alex (Sándor) and Marti Gyimesi – Alex was my singing partner and great political supporter. He had a passion for growing the most beautiful orchids. Unfortunately, Alex passed away a few years ago. We all miss him. Marti is a devoted wife, mother, and grandmother.

Alex (Sándor) and Marti Molnar – Alex was co-founder and theatrical director of the Hungarian Youth club. He was a self-made artist whose paintings were displayed in our homes for years. Marti was also a great cook and always welcomed a good cocktail. Sadly, both of them passed away in the last few years and are terribly missed.

Steve (István) and Margaret Bukkosy – Steve is my sausage-making partner. He is a great hunter and artisan. Margaret is devoted to her faith and taught and plays the organ beautifully.

Kalman and Magdi Boesze – Kalman was a dedicated educator with a respected reputation among his friends. Magdi has been very loyal to and enthusiastic about the existence of the Hungarian Club over the years.

Frank and Jean Nemeth – Frank was my painting partner and ventured with me to New York City to try our skills in the Big Apple. He was my roommate for years in Buffalo. Unfortunately, Frank passed away a few years ago. Jeannie is a great mother and wife and the life of the party. She is always smiling and knows how to have a good time, even without a little booze.

And the rest of the snowbirds in Florida, neighbors, my business colleagues, my new friends, and of course all of my Hungarian and Italian family members, who I also consider my friends.

Other Dear Friends

Dave and Carol Baer
Dr. Lajos and Eva Balogh
Jim and Joy Brandys
Dr. Emilio and Marianne Cappellucci
John and Barbara Casciani
Dale and Patti Demyanick
Wayne and Diane Forrest
Bob and Deborah Fritzinger
George and Marilyn Greenwood
Dr. Ivan and Cornelia Harangozo
Dr. Marci and Dr. Violet Haraszthy
Arpi and Eva Kolbe
Dan and Bev Malachowski

Tony and Mary Martino
Dr. Laszlo and Kati Mechtler
Dr. Steve and Kati Mechtler
Dave and Marilyn Roach
Dr. John and Jini Rubinstein
John and Karen Sanderson
Mark and Toni Sullivan
David and Pam Straitiff
Jim and Bonnie Stephen
Peter and Pam Tomasello
Dr. Andras and Connie Vari
Robert Woodrow and Lenita

Friends in Hungary

István and Judit Balogh
Miklos and Andrea Gazda
István and Andrea Halász
István and Erika Lakatos
Dr. Miklos and Anita Miskuly
Dr. László Marton and Szalontai Eniko
Nagy Erika

Péter and Niki Palkovics
György and Zsuzsa Palkovics
György Szabo
Gábor and Beatrix Vesztergombi
István Szalontai and Jakab Zsuzsa
Gábor and Usi Zentai

A weekend get-together. From left to right: Louie Nemeth, Tibi, me, and Alex Molnár.

Medieval times in Toronto, Canada. From left to right: Mary and Louie Nemeth, Maria Hegedus, me and Donna, Ildi and Tibi, Gene Hegedus, and Marti and Alex Molnar.

A party at our home. From left to right: Peter Matheisz, Steve Bukkosy, Tibi, Vince Somogyi, me, Alex Gyimesi.

In the Everglades in Florida. From left to right: Me, Miklos Gazda, and Gene Hegedus.

Frank's daughter's wedding. From left to right: Frank Nemeth, Jason Miskuly, me, Louie Nemeth.

American Friends. From left to right: Marianne and Dr. Emilio Cappellucci, Dan Malachowski, John Casciani, Wayne and Diane Forrest, Dr. John and Jini Rubinstein, Jim and Dee Dettmen, George and Marilyn Greenwood, Donna and me, Barbara Casciani, and Beverly Malachowski.

Celebrating the Fourth of July and a birthday in 1996 at the Transit Valley Country Club. From left to right: Kalman and Magdi Boesze, Judy Matheisz, Ildi and Tibi, Louie Nemeth, Marti and Alex Gyimesi, Donna, and Mary Nemeth.

At the Metropolitan Opera in New York City celebrating the sale of VTG.

A holiday gathering at Tibi's. From left to right: Tibi, Donna, me, Klári and Vincent Somogyi.

My singing partners in Hungary, Miklos Siliga and Timea Lukacs.

Celebrating with friends. Szalontai from Hungary next to my wife Donna, and his family to my right. Dr. Mechtler and his wife are on the far left.

Children's Cancer Foundation Gala in Washington, D.C. in 2009. From left to right: Erika Fedor, Judit and István Balogh, Ferenc Somogyi (Hungarian Ambassador to the United States) with his wife, Donna and me.

Wedding reception celebration. From left to right: Dr. László Mechtler, Gábor Zentai, me, Dr. Iván Harangozó, and István Szoldatits.

Dinner with friends in Kecskemet, Hungary. From left to right: Donna and the Miskuly family (Anita, Jason, Timea, Miklos, Mitya). I am on the far right.

Singing with Alex Gyimesi.

APPENDIX

M.I.C.E. Testimonials

The validity and value of M.I.C.E. is illustrated by the testimonials offered by some of our American and Hungarian students:

U.S. Student Testimonials

"I won a $40,000 entrepreneurial scholarship."

So what exactly happened as a result of M.I.C.E.? I won a $40,000 entrepreneurial scholarship. I competed in the Stern Business Competition alongside MBA students and Wall Street regulars. I've learned that "entrepreneurialism" not only entails starting a business; it means embracing an entrepreneurial spirit and passion to make your mark on the world. I just returned from Thailand, where I produced and hosted a television pilot, and am in the process of opening up another nonprofit (on top of my existing business, www.bethanybydesign.com). I have dreams that will move mountains and M.I.C.E. has given me the confidence to work towards that.

– Bethany Halbreich, class of 2007-2008

"It is a once in a lifetime opportunity."

To summarize M.I.C.E. in just a few words: "It is a once in a lifetime opportunity." It is an amazing experience on both the academic and social levels.

Having taken this course as a high school student has put me miles ahead of other students looking to pursue any business career. The classroom is unlike any class I've had because it's interactive and fun. This course introduced me to the college setting much better than my high school teachers saying: "Come on guys, this is what college is like." Being in an actual university lecture hall teaches you how to take notes in college, which is an important skill to have. The course has given me the skills necessary for being successful in college, such as how to ask questions, how to work in a team or group, and most importantly, how to learn from a professor standing in the front of the room talking on any given subject.

Socially, this class has been a phenomenal experience for me. Before this program, I couldn't put together five words in front of a group. Now I can easily stand in front of anybody and speak confidently. It also allowed me to meet and interact with students of different backgrounds, cultures, races, ethnicities, and financial status, [which] has opened my eyes to what's around me. Having done group work and activities with kids from all walks of life has given me a new appreciation for others and what they have to offer.

Using my knowledge from M.I.C.E. in talking with my managers and the owner of the company where I work, I was offered a management position right out of college. They want me to run the business when I graduate. M.I.C.E. has helped me achieve my dream and it will help you too.

– *Tyler Szczesniak, class of 2010-2011*

"If you don't have integrity, you have nothing."

The Meszaros International Center of Entrepreneurship's Ethical Entrepreneurship Training Program taught me much more than how to run a successful business. It enlightened me, giving me a new perception of how to approach life. The program taught me that, "One does not have to waiver in their ethical/moral beliefs in order to be successful in life." Since the completion of the program, I have stood by that way of thinking. I try to minimize anything that attempts to stand in the way of achieving true success and happiness. The program has opened doors for me that I never believed imaginable. I have spoken at luncheons, conducted interviews, and become an overall ambassador for the program. While saying my final goodbyes, an unfamiliar lady asked me how I felt about the program. I simply replied, "It was a life-changing experience and one of the best investments I could have possibly made for myself.

And to think, it only took sacrificing a few Saturdays during my junior year. When you ask me, 'Was it worth it'? My reply could only be, 'Most definitely!'"

– Amanda Longhorne, class of 2008-2009

"Little did I know that I was in for a life-changing experience."

When I first learned about the Meszaros International Center for Entrepreneurship, I knew I had to sign up. All my life I've been an entrepreneur of sorts, trying business venture after business venture, from trying to convert my home into a shopping mall, to attempting to organize a basketball league, to starting and financing my own record label and studio. Going in, I wasn't quite sure what to expect, but after exchanging a look, and then a smile, with Mr. Meszaros, I felt much more comfortable and eased into the program. Little did I know that I was in for a life-changing experience.

The course material, as well as the manner in which it was presented, was engaging, interesting, and strengthened my knowledge of business operations. Through this program, I not only learned the difference between an LLC and a Corporation, but also the ins and outs of every facet of business. I am a firm believer that an entrepreneur, a truly successful entrepreneur, should have, at the very least, a cursory knowledge of each department and how it works. This program taught me that, even bringing in an accounting student to help our team manage assets to come up with costs and a break-even analysis for the business plan competition. The material, however, was nothing compared to the actual final task: the business plan competition.

Coach John Wooden, who led the UCLA Bruins to ten national championships in twelve years, once said that the journey is often much more satisfying than the result. Working with my team, I learned exactly what he meant. We were all unique, we all had different strengths and weaknesses, but we shared one goal: to win. We put in long hours, trying to make our plan feasible and profitable. There were times when we didn't all see eye-to-eye, but we got it done. When the moment came, when it was our time to go up on stage with the lights on bright and all eyes on us, I could only think one thing: Game Time. The preparation we had done for that day paid off and we executed very well. There was a sense of closure and optimism as everything we had seen and been through during those six months finally came together. When we were announced the winners, it was just icing on the cake after seeing the vision come out in such a way.

I learned a lot about business in this program, but also a lot about life. I learned how to work better on a team. I learned that I was capable of stepping up into a leadership role. I learned that there is no "can't" and that perfection in the smallest details makes the big things possible. I learned all of this, but it started with me first learning that there actually is a nine o'clock on Saturday mornings...and being reminded of that fact for six long months. So to Professor Hegedus, Professor Salamone, Ms. Vanderbosch, and, of course, Mr. Meszaros, thank you for the opportunity and thank you for creating a program that is educational, interesting, fun, and worth every penny. It was the best investment I've ever made.

– George Alexander, class of 2007-2008

"The M.I.C.E.-ETP class was one of the most enriching opportunities of my life."

Originally, I was interested in law and law alone, and had my entire life planned around obtaining an undergraduate degree in political science followed by law school. My advisor was not even going to bring up the program to me, as she did not think I had any interest in business, but I was intrigued and filled out the application.

Getting into and attending the M.I.C.E. Ethical Entrepreneurship Training Program was one of the most enriching opportunities of my life. I learned a great deal about entrepreneurship and was able to meet and work with astounding individuals. While the class taught me the material, the individuals taught me about passion, work ethic, time management, and teamwork. I truly enjoyed forming the business plan and competing in the competition, and I am still in contact with my team members. I credit the M.I.C.E.-ETP with developing my interest in business, as I am now an intended business major and plan on going on to business school for my MBA.

– Jessica Yox, class of 2007-2008

"I look forward to my second son participating next year."

Just a quick follow-up on our experience with the M.I.C.E. program. Ryan is now interested in the study of business/entrepreneurism in college. Without your program, I am not sure he would have been so inclined.

He has started an Amazon reseller business, which I have previously reported to you. What you don't know is that he has 750 sales and more than 100 five star reviews. While this is not the most sophisticated business in the world, the core issues have been highlighted, including sales, customer service, responsibility, accounting, inventory, and tax issues.

Most importantly, I have been able to help Ryan make the connection that "you eat what you kill." This is an important concept for a high school senior/ college freshman to begin to understand.

Again, thanks for your program. I look forward to my second son participating next year.

– Robert Tick, parent of Ryan, class of 2011

"If you want to take your life into your own hands and succeed, M.I.C.E. is the place for you."

M.I.C.E. genuinely did what was advertised for me – it gave me the tools and foundations to run a business. Before M.I.C.E, my eBay business was barely turning a profit, but after attending the Entrepreneurship Training Program, it's thriving. Beyond this, M.I.C.E has helped me improve my public speaking skills and has pushed me to think critically. If you want to take your life into your own hands and succeed, M.I.C.E is the place for you.

– Konrad Pawlak, class of 2010-2011

Fuel the Innovation Generation

Carson Ciggia took the MICE 19-week entrepreneurship-training program as a senior in high school. In the final competition, his team wrote the winning business plan on an energy-consulting firm.

Armed with the knowledge and skills he acquired, he applied and was accepted to UB's School of Management. Soon after, he received an endowed scholarship from the school. During his freshmen and sophomore years, he launched "The Undergraduate Business Association" or "UBiz" for short. Additionally, he worked to create his own automotive detailing business during the summer months. He plans on being a corporate level executive, specifically a CEO.

His story all began at the MICE entrepreneurship-training program.

Gifts to MICE, fuel liftoffs like this one.

Let's create better students. Better entrepreneurs.

Meszaros International Center of Entrepreneurship

M.I.C.E.

A partnership with SCHOOL OF MANAGEMENT
University at Buffalo *The State University of New York*

---

*"I look back and all I can feel is incredible gratitude that
I had the chance to be a part of the M.I.C.E. program."*

I can't even believe that it has already been almost five years since I attended the M.I.C.E. program. Things have changed so much since, and I feel honored to be asked to write about the way this experience has changed me.

I was seventeen when my mom came home and told me about the M.I.C.E. program. It was quite a surprise, as she met one of the coordinators of the program while waiting in a tax office. I got very happy and excited to apply, as it sounded like something very different from the courses and programs that were available to me during that time. At that age, I felt so confused about what I wanted to do with my life, so this really sounded like a good way to start figuring things out.

M.I.C.E. was my first formal business education; therefore, it really gave me a great deal of knowledge on entrepreneurship. The guest speakers that gave presentations were very inspiring, which made me start thinking about being an entrepreneur myself one day. It all seemed like a long-term goal until we got to really come up with ideas ourselves and turned them into a business plan. This period was the most fun, as my friend and I were very serious about doing something that we could actually implement in real life. We worked day and night, which in the end paid off, as we were chosen as the winning team! This is where it all started for me. I don't think I had much confidence at the time in things I pursued in my life, but seeing that my motivation, commitment, and belief can actually make people interested, turned things around.

From the moment I won the business plan competition, I started believing that everything is possible, that it is just a matter of motivation and commitment. I saw things in a whole new light, and I did not accept people saying "no" to me. I wanted to do everything that came to mind, and I ignored those who tried to set me back. I sought more and more people who shared the same mentality as what I learned in the M.I.C.E. program. This got me very excited about seeing the world. I started traveling around Europe using the small amount of money I earned during the summers. This also opened my eyes, setting me on a totally different track than what I expected just a year before.

One time a M.I.C.E. graduate gave a presentation to inspire students to get out of the box, go see the world, and study abroad. After his presentation, I felt so inspired, but also sad because I never thought it would be possible for me to afford to do this. Slowly, slowly—while being pushed and motivated by my teammate and now my best friend—I began to research to see how to study abroad and finance it by myself. This constant research and "trying to get there" mentality got me to move to Amsterdam a year later to begin my Bachelor in economics and business degree at one of the best universities in Europe. This was not easy and smooth. It was a constant challenge and many times a struggle to sort everything out so that I could be there. I felt very disappointed many times, but still I did not give up because I knew it was possible and I knew I would achieve my goal eventually.

Three years later, I look back and all I can feel is incredible gratitude that I had the chance to be a part of the M.I.C.E. program and experience this switch in my mind that opened me up so much to the world. I feel like my life would have gone very differently if my mom had not been in that tax office five years ago and met the M.I.C.E. coordinator. These past years have been so amazing for me that I could not wish for anything better. I feel constant happiness to be where I am right now and to have been inspired by all the people who I met.

Probably the most valuable aspect of this experience for me comes down to the person who made this all possible. Laszlo Meszaros' story of going from a small Hungarian town all the way to America to be a successful businessman, and seeing him come back to give back to his community here, made me realize something very important: Never forget the people who led you to where you are and the people who inspired you to be the person you are. Always seek to share your experience with others, inspire them, change their mindsets and help them to find their own "track." I believe that one of the things that makes me the most excited about life is to give back, to help those who are stuck, those who have not been offered the same opportunities as I was offered, and to inspire them in just the same way that I was inspired by Laszlo Meszaros five years ago. And this is something I managed to figure out thanks to M.I.C.E.

I am incredibly thankful for everything that I got from this program, and I hope that other young people can also have the chance to be a part of the same experience.

Dora Jámbor, Class of 2010-2011

*"The training reflected on inner values and brought them
to the surface; I will be using these for the rest of my life"*

"If you want to become a successful businessman, you have to learn two things in life: to smoke cigars and to golf," said László Mészáros. 'Uncle Laci' is the person who perhaps has had the biggest influence on my life.

In September, 2009, I had the opportunity to participate in the almost half a year-long Ethical Entrepreneurship Training Program, organized by the M.I.C.E. Foundation, which represents the peak of Laci's lifework. I not only met a successful entrepreneur, but I learned that the most important and selfless act is sharing your knowledge with the younger generation, because they represent the biggest investment for the future.

During the training program, I learned about entrepreneurial and economical principles, which made it easy for me to complete my courses at the Budapest Corvinus University. Besides knowledge, I also gained a lot more from M.I.C.E. The training reflected on inner values and brought them to the surface; I will be using these for the rest of my life. This personal transformation made it possible for me to have an entrepreneurial attitude during my college years, for which I must thank Laci. I entered the entrepreneurial world "fully armed." A commanding presence and self-confidence in both business and my private life have shot through every facet of my life and became a crucial factor in my success later on.

As a young, purposeless student sitting on the school bench, I recall listening to Laci tell stories of his successes. The motivation inspired by his stories pushed me to move every stone and to work with endless energy and diligence during the final challenge at the end of the M.I.C.E. Program. My six-member team and I created a business plan that would have stood the test of real life situations. Our diligence and the work we invested were well worth it. Out of 120 students and 20 teams, the team that I was leading won the M.I.C.E. competition. Our prize was a visit to Laci's second home, in Buffalo, New York.

America was an unknown world for us, and going there radically changed our lives. While enjoying Laci's endless hospitality, we also had the opportunity to improve our knowledge at the University at Buffalo, to look at the operations of bigger companies, and to work with young American students. We were not only transfixed by the serious rigors of business life, but also by a feeling that was unknown to us until then: the love of our country and the insistence of our roots. We got to know the Hungarian community living in

America, who think of their home country with immeasurable love and who try to preserve their customs in their everyday lives and in their hearts.

Laci belongs to this community. He lives in Buffalo, but he often visits Hungary. We listened with childish excitement to the stories of his past, his escape, his struggle, and the story of the American Dream come true. Laci and I quickly progressed from the mentor-student relationship to a deep friendship, which I am very proud of to this day. He put his trust in me, sharing with me the stories he hid from the crowds. He allowed me to see his real self, his values. His stories about his mischievous childhood sometimes brought smiles to my face, while the stories about the horrors he experienced, the pain he went through, or his secret feelings sometimes made our time together grim while sharing a drink. "Fix whisky as the Americans do, my son, with lots of ice!" he would say at the beginning of our sessions, where he would always express some hope for the future. "Be adventurous and try your luck in America! I will be there to help you."

Balázs A. Dávid, Class of 2009-2011

INDEX

A

Áfész, 96-97
Albany, 89-90
Alexander, George, 186
Amazon, 82, 187
American Express, 119, 127
American-Hungarian Social Club, 47, 51, 59, 61, 66, 73, 145, 152
American Social Club, 60
Amherst, 146
AMOSZ (Association of Hungarian-Americans), 60
Amsterdam, 190
Aruba, 155
Association of Hungarian-Americans. *See* AMOSZ
AT&T, 112-14, 118-22
Ávós, 12

B

Badacsony, 155
Baer,
    Carol, 168, 179
    Dave, 90, 168, 179
        Data Processing, 79-80, 85-88
        Wine Making 154
    Jonathan, 154
Balaton, 176
Balázs, David A., 192
Ball State University, 161
Balogh
    Eva, 179
    István, 179, 181
    Judit, 179, 181
    Lajos, 179
Baltimore Inner Harbor, 107
Barns Hospital, 123
Bartolotti, Kim, 117
Baustar, 130. *See also* Miskuly, Miklos
Beaver Island, 63
Bethlehem Steel, 52-53, 56
Boeing, 119, 127
Boesze, Kalman and Magdi, 179
Bosnia, 155, 168
Boston, 111, 172
Boulder, 120, 161
Boulevard Towers, 146
Boyd, Donna, 117
Brandys, Jim and Joy, 179
Budapest, 65, 138, 155,
    Business in, 130-31
    Traveling with the Sullivans, 107
    Super Marathon in, 171-73
Budapest Corvinus University, 191
Buffalo Police Department, 85-87
Bukkosy Margaret and Steve (István), 179-80
Bükks Mountains, 6-7

C

Cako, Csaba and Bela 68
Calasanctius High School, 60, 139, 148
Campbell, Dave, 90
Canada, 34, 151, 155, 180
    CIS in, 105
    Hungarian Youth Club in, 62
    Muskoka Lake, 67, 102, 149

cancer, 122-24, 162
Canisius College, 151
Canisius High School, 151
Cappellucci Emilio and Marianne, 179
Casciani, Barbara and John, 179-80
Catholic Charities, 46-47, 49, 51
   for immigration, 34
Central Police Services. *See* CPS
Chambers, John, 128
Ciggia, Carson, 188
Ciminelli, Frank, 110
CIS, 104-9, 111
Cisco, 118, 128. *See also* Chambers,
   John
City of Buffalo Police Department, 87
Coast Guard, 107
colon cancer, 77-78
Colvin Avenue, 54
communist, 10-11, 24
   Hungary, 12-13, 15, 17, 19, 21, 196
   party, 11, 13, 21
   regime, 12, 59, 83, 175
Com-Pro, 113,
   Birth of, 93-96
   Buffalo branch, 109
   Growth, 103-11
   Mistakes made in, 100-101
   Sale of, 107
   VTG and Com-Pro, 116-17
Computer Task Group *See* CTG
Continent Information Services, 104
Cornwall Avenue, 49-50
Corvinus University, 138
County Executive Regan, 88. *See also*
   Regan, Ed
County Legislature, 88
Croatia, 5, 16, 18-19, 27-31, 34, 37, 62,
   155
Crumlish, Bud, 105
Csákánydoroszló, 6
Csorna, Hungary, 3
Csülkös Bableves (Bean Soup), 86
CTG (Computer Task Group), 80,
   85-91, 93-94, 121, 145

D

Danube River, 172
Dean's Advisory Council, 135
Delaware Avenue, 51
Delevan Avenue, 49
Demyanick Dale and Patty, 172-73, 179
Denies, Steve, 117
Dépé, 59
Depot Restaurant, 145
Dettmen, Dee, 180
Dingens Street, 145
Dixon, Scott, 139
Donofrio, Rosaria Ann (Donna) *See*
      Donna Meszaros
   brothers and cousins, 63, 84, 156, 178
   family, 145, 147, 149, 156-57, 164
   home, 167
   married life, 145-49
   matron of honor, 148
   mother, as a, 152, 154, 156-61
   speech by, 110
Drucker, Peter, 123
Dubai, 168
DuPont, 108-9, 111-12, 119, 127

E

East Avenue, 61
Eckerson, Nancy Jo, 177
Egger, Laszlo, 172
Ellis Island, 41
Elmwood Avenue, 196
Enczmann, Eva, 138
entrepreneur, 54, 92, 99, 113, 135-37,
      139, 141, 177, 183, 185-86, 189
   accomplishments, 196
   ethics, 135
   Foundation, 139
   Training Program, 135, 187
   ventures, 133, 135-39, 141, 185-86,
      189, 196
equity, 125
   sharing, 132
   sweat, 112
Erdődy Pál, Gróf, 3
Erie Canal, 151
Erie County

Community College, 76
Executive, 87
Sheriff's Department, 87
Ernst & Young, 107
Ethical Entrepreneurship Training
    Program, 184, 186
Executive Regan, 88

F
family
    background, 61
    extended, 165-67, 169, 171, 173
    gatherings, 167
    history, 83
    vacations, 151
Farkas, Jack, 54
F.B.I., 87, 89, 102
Fedor, Erika, 181
Finland, 155, 168-69
Finnegan, Paul, 168
Florida, 151, 155, 179-80
Fonyod, 138
Forgach, Peter, 165, 173
Forrest, Diane and Wayne, 179-80
Frankfurt, 84
Fritzinger
    Deborah, 179
    Robert H., 108, 111-13, 122, 129, 179

G
Gazda
    Andrea, 179
    Miklos, 179-80
General Taylor, 43
Georgian Bay, 65
Germany, 6, 9, 36-37, 98
God, 7-11, 14-15, 25, 27, 30, 33, 37,
    42-43, 45, 49-50, 98, 102, 152, 173,
    175
Google, 137
Gorica Vineyard, 27
Gourmet Club, 90
Greenwood
    George, 117, 169-70, 179
    Marilyn, 169, 179-80
Grove, Andy, 116, 123. See also Intel
Güssing, 28-29

Gyimesi, Alex and Marti, 178-81
Győr, 81, 84, 97-98

H
Halász
    Andrea, 179
    István, 130, 179
Halbreich, Bethany, 183
Harangozó
    Cornelia, 179
    Iván, 165, 179, 181
Haraszthy, Marci and Violet, 179
Harlem, 55-56
Hartmann, Heather, 139
Havas
    Frank, 64
    Kathy, 63-64, 86
    Family, 65
Haver-Varga, Marianna, 138
Hawaii Pacific University, 161
Hegedus,
    Gene (Jeno), 60, 136, 139, 178, 180,
        186
    Maria, 178, 180
Hegyeshalom, 81
Heroes' Square in Budapest, 172-73
Hertel Avenue, 61
Heuser, Tim, 117
Honolulu, 161
Hudson River, 44
Hungarian Organizations in Buffalo, 60

I
IBM, 79-80, 89, 103
Intel, 116-17, 129
Iron Curtain, 22, 27, 81

J
Jámbor, Dora, 190, 196
Jáni, János, 33
Jewish Community Center, 127, 151
J.H. Williams, 56-57, 73-75
John Deere, 119, 127
Juci, Bogar, 64
Juhasz, 46
Jurasits, Félix and Rudi, 33

K

Kalp, Ron, 126
Kapitany, John, 62
Kaun, Connie, 110
Kecskemet, 130, 181
Kenmore, 51
Kisgazda Párt, 11
Kiskőrös, 84
Kodak, 95
Kolbe
  Arpi, 155, 166-67, 179
  Eva, 179
  Mary, 167
Körmend, 96
Körmendi Township, 6
Kraus Shingle Panel Company, 49-50
Kulcsar, Viki, 138
Kúti, Erzsébet, 3-9, 11, 13, 15-17, 21-23,
  25, 43, 46, 63-64, 67, 69, 74, 82-84,
  160-61, 178-79

L

Lady of Mariazell, 33-34
Lakatos, Erika and István, 179
Lake Balaton, 155
Lake Erie, 63
Letchworth State Park, 63, 156
Longhorne, Amanda, 185
Lou Gehrigs disease, 122
Lucent, 118-19
Lukacs, Timea, 181

M

Magyar Ház. *See* American Social Club
Malachowski, Beverly and Dan, 179-180
Manhattan, 44
Marian Shrine, 34
Marine Midland Bank, 93
Marks, Randy, 80, 86-87, 90
Martino,
  Mary, 172-73, 179
  Tony, 172-73, 179
  Susan Burke, 173
Marton, László, 179
Matheisz
  Judy, 178, 180

Peter, 90, 172-73, 180
McQuay, Greg, 117, 122
Mechtler, Kati, László and Steve, 179
Meszaros
  Cheri, 155, 160-62, 164
  Christopher, 92, 110, 122, 129, 148-
    52, 151-52, 154-57, 159-62, 164,
    167
  Donna, 98, 102, 107, 110, 145-49,
    152, 155-56, 158-61, 164, 166-70,
    172-73, 180-81
    See also Donofrio, Rosaria Ann
    (Donna)
  Erika, 110, 151-52, 154-56, 159, 161-
    62, 164
    See also Wayo, Erika Meszaros
Mészáros
  Akos, 156
  Ildi, 3, 9, 11, 13, 68, 84, 148, 156-57,
    178, 180
  Katalin, 3, 16
  Klári, 3-4, 9, 11, 13, 15-16, 82-83, 96,
    98, 156, 178, 181
  László, 3, 5, 8, 11, 13, 15, 46, 179
  Margit, 4-5, 11, 145
  Nénje, 16, 18, 43-44, 149, 156
Meszaros International Center for
    Entrepreneurship. *See* M.I.C.E.
Metropolitan Opera in New York City,
    180
M.I.C.E, 117, 133-41, 163, 176, 178,
    183-84, 186, 189-91
Microsoft, 118-19
Middlesex Avenue, 54-55
Miller, Joe, 117
Miskuly,
  Anita, 179, 181
  family, 181
  Jason, 180
  Miklos, 179
Mitel, 118, 121-22, 127
Molnár, Alex and Marti, 61, 178, 180
M&T Bank, 95
Muskoka Lake, 65, 67, 102

N

Nádasy, Kathy, 62
Nadler, Doctor, 77
Nagy
    Erizsi, 171
    Erika, 179
    Sándor, 51, 171, 178
Natural Microsystems. *See* NMS
Nemeth,
    Bandi, 33
    Frank, 62, 179-80
    Jean, 179
    Louie (Lajos), 47-49, 51-52, 54, 56,
        59, 62, 65, 178, 180
    Mary, 178, 180
New York City, 37, 42, 44-45, 55, 59,
    165, 179-80
NMS (Natural Microsystems), 126-27
Northern Telecom, 113-14, 118-21

O

Obuda, Hungary, 172
Ontario, 61, 63

P

Palkovics
    György, 179
    Nikolett, 166, 179
    Péter, 165-66, 179
    Zsuzsa, 179
Pannonhalma, 83-84, 96, 98
Papp, Gabor, 68
Pawlak, Konrad, 187
Pax Hotel, 96-97, 173
PBX (Private Branch Exchange), 113,
    119, 121, 127-28
Phalen, Doctor, 77-78
Piarista High School, 138
Police Department, *see* Buffalo Police
    Department
Pongrác, Gábor, 13
Portugal, 155, 168
Private Branch Exchange *see* PBX

R

Regan, Ed, 87
Remington Rand, 49
Richmond, 159
Riverside High School, 54
Roach
    David, 122, 179
    Marilyn, 179
Roswell Park Cancer Institute, 73-75, 77,
    79-80, 85-87, 135, 159, 162
Rotterdam, 31
Rubinstein, Jini and John, 179-80

S

Saint Gregory, 167
Saint Steven's Day, 62
Sanderson John and Karen, 179
Sándor, Alex, 178
Santo Domingo, 170
Schleifer, Bertalan and Margit, 4
Sherkston, 63
Siberia, 60
Siemens, 118
Silicon Valley, 111-13, 115-17, 119, 121,
    123, 125, 127, 129
Siliga, Miklos, 181
Skrapits, Father John, 33, 46, 61, 68, 148
Smith, Joe, 108
Somogyi
    Ferenc, 181
    Vincent, 178, 180-81
    Klári, 178
Stadard, Fred, 168
State Hermitage Museum, 168
Statler Hotel, 161, 164
St. Elizabeth's Hungarian Catholic
    Church, 63, 148
Stephen, Bonnie and Jim, 179
Stern Business Competition, 183
St. Gregory, 152, 167
St. Joseph's Cathedral, 161
St. Louis, 123-24
St. Martin, 168
St. Mary, 27
St. Peter and Paul's Day, 16
St. Petersburg, 168

Straitiff
   David, 109, 111-16, 120, 122, 125, 179
      See also VoiceBridge
   Pam, 179
Sullivan
   Mark, 106-7
   Mark and Toni, 107, 179
Switzerland, 155
Syracuse, 104, 107
Szabo
   György, 179
   Sandor, 49, 51
Szakacs Bella, 73
Szalontai
   Eniko, 179
   István, 24, 179, 181
Szczesniak, Tyler, 184
Szentpéterfa, 3-6, 11, 13-14, 16, 18-20, 24, 27-29, 31-32, 38, 46, 55, 165
Szoldatits, Alfonz, 21, 24, 33
Szombathely, 13-14, 16-17, 19-23

T

Tampa, 95, 109
Tarótfa, 4
Tatabánya, 130
Teleki, Kornel, 62, 64
Thailand, 183
Tick, Robert, 187
Tokaj, 155
Tomasello, Peter, 90, 94-95, 100-101, 104-6, 165-66, 178-79
Toney, Monica, 117, 139
Transit Valley Country Club, 163, 180
tuberculosis, 3-4
Tutuska, Andy, 51-52, 116

U

UB (University at Buffalo), 135, 139, 165, 188, 191
   School of Management, 135
USNS General Harry Taylor, 36

V

Vari, Dr. Andras and Connie, 179
Vas County, 3, 6
Vesztergombi, Gábor, 179
Vienna, 81, 171-72
VoiceBridge, 109, 111-14, 116, 118-19, 121-22, 126
Voicemail Association (VMA), 168
Voice-over-IP (VOIP), 117, 128
Voice Technologies Group. *See* VTG
Vörösvár, 31, 34
VTG (Voice Technologies Group), 111-23, 125-29, 135, 151, 160, 180

W

Wagner, Terry, 110
Washington, 87, 89-90, 181
Wayo
   Joseph, 26, 155-56, 161-62, 164, 177
   Mike, 164
   Erika, 107, 124, 153, 157, 160, 162-63, 166
      See also Meszaros, Erika
   Joan, 164
Wegman, Terry, 173
Wehle School, Richard J., 151
Williamsville, 167
Williamsville East High School, 152
Wolcott Street, 56
Wooden, Coach John, 185
Woodrow
   Lenita, 179
   Robert, 104-6, 179
Worcester, 151
World War II, 47, 57, 59

Y

Yox, Jessica, 186
Yugoslavians, 37

Z

Zentai, Gábor and Usi, 179, 181
Zimics, József, 33
Zsuzsa, Jakab, 179